EDEXCEL
GERMANY 1919–1945
FOR SHP GCSE

Dale Banham

Christopher Culpin

Acknowledgements

Photo credits

Cover © Hulton-Deutsch Collection/Corbis; **p.2** © bpk/Bayerische Staatsbibliothek/Heinrich Hoffmann; **p.6** © bpk; **p.7** © akg-images; **p.10** *b* © Süddeutsche Zeitung Photo/SZ Photo; **p.12** *t* © bpk, *b* © akg-images; **p.13** *t* © Ullsteinbild/TopFoto, *b* © bpk/Heinrich Hoffmann; **p.15** *t & b* © Bettman/Corbis; **p.26** © akg-images; **p.29** *t* © Ullsteinbild/TopFoto, *b* © akg-images; **p.31** © Ullsteinbild/TopFoto; **p.41** © bpk/Bayerische Staatsbibliothek/Heinrich Hoffmann; **p.46** © bpk/SBB; **p.53** *t & b* © ullstein bild – Frentz; **p.54** *t* © ullstein bild – Frentz, *b* © akg-images; **p.55** *l* © 2008 IBL Collections/Mary Evans Picture Library, *r* © Süddeutsche Zeitung Photo/Scherl; **p.56** *t* © Süddeutsche Zeitung Photo/Scherl; **p.57** *t & b* © akg-images; **p.59** *t* © akg-images, *b* © Hulton-Deutsch Collection/CORBIS; **p.60** Courtesy of the Army Art Collection, U.S. Army Center of Military History; p.**65** © Ullsteinbild/TopFoto; **p.66** *tl* © Süddeutsche Zeitung Photo/SZ Photo, *tr* © akg-images, *b* © akg-images; **p.67** © Ullsteinbild/TopFoto; **p.68** *b* © Ullsteinbild/TopFoto; **p.75** © Bundesarchiv, Plak 003-002-046, Graphiker: René Ahrlé; **p.76** © Süddeutsche Zeitung Photo/Scherl; **p.77** © Bundesarchiv, Bild 146-1973-060-19, Fotograf: o.Ang.; **p.78** © Institut fur Stadtgeschichte, Frankfurt am Main; **p.79** *l* © bpk/Germin, *r* © Süddeutsche Zeitung Photo/Scherl; **p.80** © akg-images; **p.81** © bpk; **p.86** *l* © akg-images, *r* © World History Archive/Alamy; **p.87** *t* © akg-images/ullstein bild, *b* © Image bank WW2 – Netherlands Institute for War Documentation; **p.88** © akg-images/Michael Teller.

Text credits

p.15 K. Heiden, *Der Führer: Hitler's Rise to Power* (Pordes, 1967); **p.40** E. A Butler, *Darkness over Germany* (Longman, 1943); **p.88** Rudolph Höss, *Death Dealer: The Memoirs of the SS Kommandant at Auschwitz* (DaCapo Press, 1996).

Every effort has been made to trace all copyright holders, but if any have been inadvertently overlooked the Publishers will be pleased to make the necessary arrangements at the first opportunity.

The Schools History Project

Set up in 1972 to bring new life to history for students aged 13–16, the Schools History Project continues to play an innovatory role in secondary history education. From the start, SHP aimed to show how good history has an important contribution to make to the education of a young person. It does this by creating courses and materials which both respect the importance of up-to-date, well-researched history and provide enjoyable learning experiences for students.

Since 1978 the Project has been based at Trinity and All Saints University College Leeds. It continues to support, inspire and challenge teachers through the annual conference, regional courses and website: www.schoolshistoryproject.org.uk.
The Project is also closely involved with government bodies and awarding bodies in the planning of courses for Key Stage 3, GCSE and A level.

Although every effort has been made to ensure that website addresses are correct at time of going to press, Hodder Education cannot be held responsible for the content of any website mentioned in this book. It is sometimes possible to find a relocated web page by typing in the address of the home page for a website in the URL window of your browser.

Hachette UK's policy is to use papers that are natural, renewable and recyclable products and made from wood grown in sustainable forests. The logging and manufacturing processes are expected to conform to the environmental regulations of the country of origin.

Orders: please contact Bookpoint Ltd, 130 Milton Park, Abingdon, Oxon OX14 4SB. Telephone: +44 (0)1235 827720. Fax: +44 (0)1235 400454. Lines are open 9.00a.m.–5.00p.m., Monday to Saturday, with a 24-hour message answering service. Visit our website at www.hoddereducation.co.uk.

Typeset in 11/13 pt Palatino Light
Layouts by Ian Foulis
Artwork by Art Construction, Richard Duszczak, Jon Davis/Linden Artists, Janek Matysiak, Tony Randell, Steve Smith
Printed in Dubai

A catalogue record for this title is available from the British Library

ISBN 978 1 444 12310 4

Contents

You probably recognise the man in the middle of this picture, the focus of everyone's attention: Adolf Hitler. He became ruler of Germany in 1933 and remained in power until 1945. The people in the picture seem to be very pleased with him. Yet Hitler eventually hurtled Germany into war and murdered millions of people. By 1945 his country was in ruins and his people were starving.

How could this happen? How could the intelligent, educated people of a modern, democratic country let Hitler take over? And what happened to them once he had? These are the **big questions** that you are going to answer in this book. To answer them you need to study the period in some depth. That is why this is called a depth study.

A depth study:

- concentrates on a short period of history – in this case 27 years, from 1919 to 1945

- looks at *one* particular place at that time – in this case Germany

- looks at the lives of ordinary people (children, women and men) – not just at famous or powerful people

- studies people's feelings and motives – what made them tick and why they did what they did.

What are the best ways to prepare for your GCSE exams?

Good revision and planning will help you do well at GCSE. We will help you using the two important features below.

 smarter revision

The Smarter Revision toolkit

The toolkit helps you remember important information in different ways and link it all together – which improves your written answers.

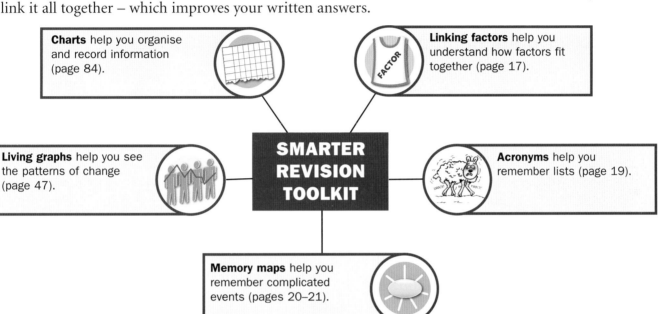

Charts help you organise and record information (page 84).

Linking factors help you understand how factors fit together (page 17).

Living graphs help you see the patterns of change (page 47).

SMARTER REVISION TOOLKIT

Acronyms help you remember lists (page 19).

Memory maps help you remember complicated events (pages 20–21).

 meet the examiner

Practise the skills that you need to succeed in Edexcel GCSE examinations:

- **Examine that question.** Find out what examiners are really looking for (see page 27).

- **Improve that answer.** Spot the good points and see if you can improve the bad points (see page 35).

- **Warning!** Learn how to avoid common mistakes (see page 50).

1.1 What problems did the Weimar Republic face?

Germany emerged from its defeat in the First World War with a new government, called the Weimar Republic. It faced a lot of serious problems. It only just survived. Your task will be to examine these problems and decide which was the most threatening.

Why did Germany need a new government in 1918?

Since 1888 Germany had been ruled by Kaiser (Emperor) Wilhelm II. Although Germany had a parliament, called the Reichstag, it was the Kaiser, a **strong leader**, who had most of the power. He chose ministers to help him run the country. He made sure that they would do what he wanted. If they did not, he would sack them.

By the autumn of 1918 the Kaiser was in big trouble. For four years Germany had been fighting in the First World War. It now faced certain defeat. The German army was retreating and people in Germany faced **starvation**.

The Allies (Britain, France and the USA) would only make peace with Germany if it became more democratic. This meant getting rid of the Kaiser and setting up a new government. Throughout Germany there were **violent uprisings** against the Kaiser. Eventually, he was forced to flee to the Netherlands. Germany became a republic.

Friedrich Ebert became the new **democratically elected** leader of Germany. Ebert was leader of the Social Democrats, the largest party in the Reichstag.

How was the Weimar Republic governed?

In 1919 there was a general election. Friedrich Ebert became the President. There was too much violence in Berlin, the capital, for the new government to meet there, so it met in the town of Weimar. The government was therefore called the Weimar Republic.

During 1919 a new constitution was drawn up. This set rules for how Germany would be governed. As you can see from the diagram below, it was very different from the old system, under the Kaiser. In fact, the Weimar constitution was one of the most democratic systems of government in the world.

THE WEIMAR CONSTITUTION

THE PRESIDENT
- Elected every seven years
- Controlled the armed forces
- Stayed out of the day-to-day running of the country
- In an emergency he could make laws without going through the Reichstag (Parliament)

appointed

THE CHANCELLOR
- Responsible for the day-to-day running of the country
- Chosen from the Reichstag by the President
- Like a Prime Minister

needed the support of more than half of

THE REICHSTAG (Parliament)
- Voted on new laws
- Members elected every four years, through a system called PR (proportional representation). This system gave small parties a chance to have a say in Parliament

was elected by

THE GERMAN PEOPLE
- Elected the President and the members of the Reichstag
- All men and women over the age of 20 could vote
- All adults had equal rights and the right of free speech

Discuss

1 What do you like about the Weimar constitution?
2 What weaknesses can you see in it?
3 What differences can you spot between the way the Weimar Republic was governed and the way the country you live in is governed?

Coming up...

This constitution looks promising, doesn't it? Unfortunately for the new Weimar Republic it was set up at a very difficult time. As you will see in the rest of this chapter, the new Republic faced serious problems.

Problems, problems, problems!

You are now going to study, in detail, five problems that the Weimar Republic faced. Do not think that each problem went away as another appeared. In fact, new problems combined with old problems. More and more problems built up. Together these problems threatened to destroy the Weimar Republic.

It was the end of the First World War that set the ball rolling…

On the next 10 pages you will analyse the problems which combined to weaken the Weimar Republic. On pages 16–17 you will assess the importance of each problem and show the links between them.

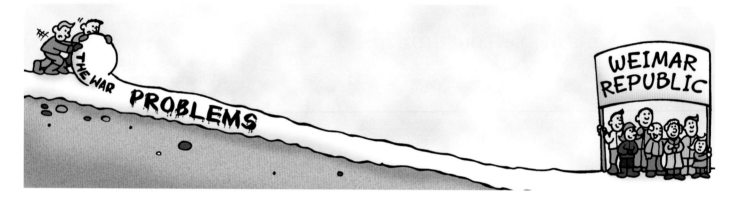

PROBLEM 1: DEFEAT IN THE FIRST WORLD WAR – THE 'STAB IN THE BACK'

Within days of taking over, the new government had to sign an armistice that ended the fighting in the First World War. The leaders of the Republic had little choice but to sign this – the German army was retreating and people at home faced starvation.

However, not all Germans saw it this way. Just a few months earlier the war had been going well. The German army had been advancing and victory seemed possible. During the war the Kaiser had not announced any bad news to the German people, so the peace, in November 1918, had come as a shock.

People were now very bitter and were looking for someone to blame. A simple explanation for the defeat quickly spread. The great German army had been 'stabbed in the back' by the new government.

▲ Happy German children riding on a gun carriage as the soldiers come home following the signing of the armistice on 11 November 1918.

THE 'STAB IN THE BACK' MYTH SUMMARISED

The German army was a great fighting force. Our brave, patriotic soldiers were not defeated on the battlefield. Our army could have won the war. The politicians are to blame. They wanted to stop the war. They caused unrest among civilians and damaged the morale of our troops. They have **stabbed our great country in the back**. This government is full of criminals and the armistice is a disgrace.

Clearly, Germany's defeat in the First World War was not the fault of the leaders of the new Republic. However, this did not matter. Many people in Germany believed that they had been stabbed in the back by the new government. **They blamed the leaders of the Weimar Republic, not the army generals, for Germany's defeat.** As you can see from the poster below, opponents of the Weimar Republic used this to their advantage to weaken support for the leaders of the Weimar Republic.

Source 1

◄ A German National Party election poster, from 1924. The words at the bottom of the poster say: 'Who stabbed the German armies in the back in the World War? Whose fault is it that our People and Fatherland must sink so deep into misfortune?'

Discuss

Why might many Germans have wanted to believe in the idea that their soldiers had been 'stabbed in the back' by the leaders of the Weimar Republic?

PROBLEM 2: THE TREATY OF VERSAILLES

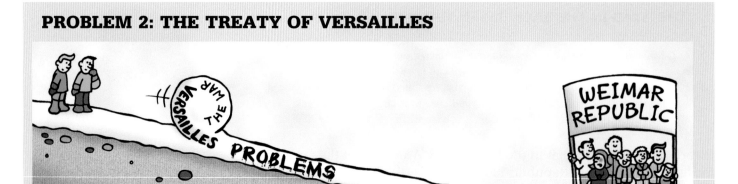

The First World War ended with the signing of the armistice in November 1918. However, it took until June 1919 for the Allies to agree on a peace treaty. The new German government was not invited to the discussions. These discussions took place at Versailles in France so the treaty was called the Treaty of Versailles.

What did the German people hope for?

The German people hoped for a fair treaty. There were three reasons for this.

1 The Allies said that they wanted a more democratic Germany. That is what we have created. The Kaiser has gone. **Our new government needs support**, not punishment. The Allies will not punish us for what the Kaiser did.

2 President Wilson of the USA is on our side. He has already said that the treaty should not be too hard on us. **Wilson has come up with Fourteen Points** that will form the basis of a fair treaty. France and Britain will have to listen to him.

3 Germany did not start the First World War. **It is not to blame for the war**. All the countries involved should take a share of the blame. We do not expect to be punished for a war we did not start!

What did the German people get?

The terms of the Treaty of Versailles came as a real shock to the German people. France and Britain put pressure on President Wilson and forced him to accept a treaty that was designed to seriously weaken Germany.

Discuss

1 Which parts of the Treaty were most likely to make the German people feel: angry, humiliated, insecure?
2 Which parts of the Treaty were most likely to cause problems for the Weimar Republic?

THE TERMS OF THE TREATY

PART 1: LAND
- Germany lost 13 per cent of its land (and about 6 million people living there).
- This lost land had important raw materials, such as coal.
- Germany was split in two. This was to give Poland access to the sea.
- German troops were not allowed in the Rhineland. This was to make the French feel safe from a German attack.
- All Germany's overseas colonies were taken away.

PART 2: ARMY
- The German army was to be reduced to just 100,000.
- The navy was cut to 15,000 sailors and only six battleships.
- Germany was not allowed submarines, tanks or an air force.

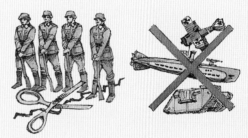

PART 3: BLAME
- In the 'war guilt' clause, Germany was blamed for the war.
- This enabled the Allies to demand compensation from Germany for all the damage that had been caused.

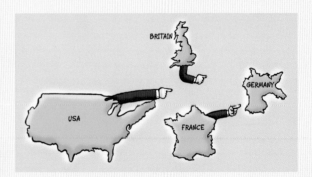

PART 4: MONEY
- Germany had to pay reparations. Most of the money would go to France and Belgium.
- At Versailles no sum was fixed. But in 1921 the Allies fixed the total amount that Germany had to pay at £6600 million.

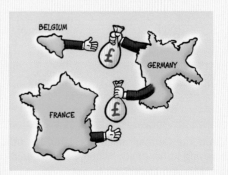

9

How did the German people react?

The German people felt humiliated by the Treaty of Versailles. They hated the Treaty, and the people who made it.

The German government did not like this Treaty either. However, they had little choice but to accept it. The Allies threatened to restart the war if they did not sign the peace treaty.

However, opponents of the Weimar Republic now blamed the new government for signing the Treaty. To them, the fact that the government had signed the Treaty showed how weak they were and reinforced the view that they had stabbed Germany in the back.

◀ This cartoon appeared in a German newspaper in July 1919. It was called 'Clemenceau the Vampire'. Clemenceau was the leader of France who wanted a treaty that would cripple Germany. The woman on the bed represents Germany.

Source 3

▲ This cartoon appeared in a German magazine, in 1919, attacking the Treaty. The mother is saying to her child: 'When we have paid one hundred billion marks then I can give you something to eat.'

Activity 1

Imagine that you are an editor of a German newspaper in 1919 that is against the government. Design a front page reporting on the Treaty of Versailles. It should include:

*   a powerful headline that will sum up the mood of the German people
*   a summary of the key points of the Treaty
*   a description of how German people feel about the Treaty. Aim to get across the feelings of shock, anger and humiliation
*   an explanation of why people feel this way. You could include some quotes from your readers
*   a cartoon. You could use one of the cartoons here, or you could research or draw another cartoon of your own
*   a comment on why the leaders of the Weimar Republic are to blame for the Treaty.

PROBLEM 3: POLITICAL VIOLENCE

The Weimar Republic was democratic – people had the right to choose their government. However, some groups did not think that this was the best way to run Germany. These extremist parties wanted to tear the Weimar Republic apart.

On pages 12–13 you will find details of four extreme groups that used violence to try to overthrow the Weimar Republic. They all harmed the Republic a bit because they reduced the confidence the German people had in their new government. But you must decide which group represented the *biggest threat*.

Your task is to produce a **secret report** for the Weimar government on each of the groups. Your report should:

1 Briefly describe each group and explain how it tried to take over.
2 Examine the strengths and weaknesses of each group. Consider:
   • leadership
   • support
   • organisation
   • how close it came to taking over the country.
3 End by giving each group a danger rating out of 5 (5 a serious threat; 1 a small threat). Make sure you explain your rating.

EXTREME, LEFT-WING PARTIES
Communist Party
• They believed that they should run the country on behalf of the workers.

EXTREME, RIGHT-WING PARTIES
Nazi Party
German National Party
• They believed that Germany should have one strong leader, whom everyone should obey.

Left-wing violence

Which extremist political group was the

THREAT 1: THE SPARTACIST RISING, 1919

Who?
The Spartacist League. A Communist group set up by Rosa Luxemburg and Karl Liebknecht.

Why?
Spartacists wanted a full-scale Communist revolution like the recent Russian Revolution of 1917. They did not trust the new government. They thought that Ebert would not improve the lives of working people.

What?
In January 1919 workers were protesting throughout Germany. The Spartacists tried to turn this into a revolution. In Berlin they took over the government's newspaper and telegraph headquarters. They hoped protesters would join them and take over other buildings, but this did not happen. The government ordered the army to stop the uprising. The army was helped by units of the Freikorps. These units were made up of ex-soldiers

Spartacists defending the captured newspaper offices

who were anti-Communist. In the fighting that followed over 100 workers were killed.

Success?
The uprising was badly planned. The Spartacists did not get support from other left-wing groups. Rosa Luxemburg was captured by the Freikorps and shot. Her body was dumped in a Berlin canal. Karl Liebknecht was also murdered. Without their main leaders the Spartacists were defeated.

THREAT 2: THE RED RISING IN THE RUHR, 1920

Who?
Groups of workers led by members of the Communist Party.

Why?
Many German workers were angry about bad pay and bad working conditions. Workers had been protesting throughout 1919.

What?
In 1920 a Communist 'Red Army' of 50,000 workers occupied the Ruhr region of Germany and took control of its raw materials. This was one of Germany's main industrial areas. The German army, with the help of the Freikorps, crushed the rising. Over 1000 workers were killed.

The Communist Red Army preparing to fight the Freikorps in 1920

Success?
The Communist Party had weak leadership. They did not have a clear plan. Protests did not have widespread, committed support. For the next few years there were lots of demonstrations and strikes, but unrest never seriously threatened the Weimar government's control of Germany.

Right-wing violence

biggest threat to the Weimar Republic?

THREAT 3: THE KAPP PUTSCH, 1920

Who?
Freikorps units, led by Wolfgang Kapp.

Why?
In 1920 the government ordered that the Freikorps brigades be disbanded. It had little need for them now that left-wing groups had been crushed.

What?
Around 12,000 Freikorps marched to Berlin. The government was forced to flee. The Freikorps put forward Kapp as the new leader of Germany.

Success?
Kapp and the Freikorps failed to win much

Kapp Putsch troops in Berlin

support. In Berlin, workers went on strike in protest at the putsch. This made it impossible for Kapp to rule. After four days he fled from Berlin and Ebert's government returned.

THREAT 4: THE MUNICH PUTSCH, 1923

Who?
The Nazi Party (led by Adolf Hitler) and General Ludendorff (a popular First World War hero who had been involved in the Kapp Putsch). The Nazis had 55,000 members and their own private army called the SA.

Why?
Adolf Hitler and the Nazi Party believed that democracy only led to weak government. They thought that there should be only one political party, with one leader.

What?
The Nazis planned to take over the government and set up General Ludendorff as leader of Germany. They started in Munich. Hitler and 600 of his SA burst into a meeting where the leader of Bavaria (Kahr) was speaking. They forced Kahr to promise to support their plan.

Success?
The putsch had not been properly planned. Kahr was allowed to leave the beer hall, and

Putsch leaders pose before their trial. General Ludendorff and Hitler are in the centre.

the following day he withdrew his support. The German government responded quickly. They ordered the army to crush the revolt. When armed Nazis marched to a military base in Munich they were met by the armed police and soldiers. In the fighting that followed fourteen Nazis were killed. The leaders of the putsch were arrested and Hitler was sent to prison for five years. He was released after just nine months, but during this time the Nazis nearly fell apart without their leader.

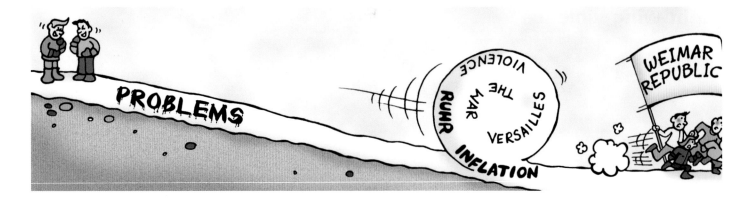

PROBLEM 4: INVASION OF THE RUHR

Germany struggled to keep up with the reparation payments to the Allies. In 1922 Germany announced that it could not afford to pay reparations for the next three years. France did not believe this and was determined to make Germany pay. In 1923 60,000 French and Belgian troops marched into the Ruhr, an important industrial area of Germany. They seized control of all mines, factories and railways. They took supplies from shops and set up machine-gun posts in the streets.

What problems did this cause?

The German government told workers not to co-operate with the French. All workers went on strike. This policy was known as passive resistance. It was a non-violent protest against the invasion. Despite this, 140 Germans were killed in clashes with troops.

The workers who went on strike received money from the German government, to support their families. This cost the government a lot of money. To make matters worse, no money was coming in from the Ruhr, one of Germany's main industrial areas. The government was running very short of money.

As you can see from the next column, the government's solution to this problem just created an even bigger problem.

PROBLEM 5: HYPER-INFLATION

The government becomes very short of money.

The government prints more money to pay workers and to pay its debts.

1000 M   1000 M

The more money printed, the less it is worth.

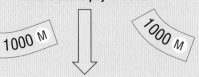

People lose confidence in the German mark.

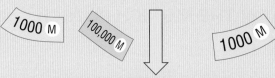

Prices rise at an incredible rate (hyper-inflation).
In January 1919 one US dollar is worth nearly 9 marks.
By November 1923 one dollar is worth 200 billion marks.
At one stage an egg costs 80 million marks and a glass of beer 150 million marks.

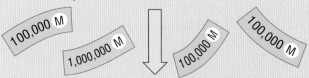

By November 1923 the German mark is worthless.

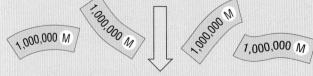

Source 4

▲ German children, in 1923, show how many German marks are equal to one US dollar

How did hyper-inflation affect the German people?

Hyper-inflation affected people in different ways, as you can see from the table below. However, there were far more losers than winners. For most people in Germany, in 1923, life became very difficult.

HYPER-INFLATION	
Winners	Losers
People in debt found it easier to pay off their loans.	People with savings were the biggest losers. The value of what they had saved fell drastically. Pensioners were badly hit. In 1919, 6000 marks was a small fortune. By 1923 it would not even buy a stamp for a letter!
Businessmen found it easier to pay back money they had borrowed to build up their businesses.	Workers found that wage increases did not keep up with rising prices.

There were major food shortages because farmers did not want to sell food for worthless money. There were deaths from starvation. Some people turned to crime because life was so hard.

Source 6 shows how everyday life was affected.

Source 5

▲ A woman using banknotes to start her fire, 1923

Source 6

An account written by someone who lived through hyper-inflation in Germany

On Friday afternoons in 1923, very long lines of workers waited outside the pay windows of the big German factories . . . until at last they reached the pay window and received a bag full of paper banknotes.

The figures on the banknotes could be as high as 18 trillion marks.

As soon as they got their money the workers began running to food stores. Here there were slow queues. If you got there first a half kilo of sugar could be bought for 2 million marks. If you were at the back of the queue, by the time you got to the counter, 2 million marks would only buy you a quarter of a kilo of sugar.

People carried their money around in sacks or prams. Life was madness, nightmare, desperation and chaos.

Did hyper-inflation damage the Weimar Republic more than any other problem?

The Weimar Republic was seriously weakened by hyper-inflation. Millions lost their savings and there was widespread hunger. As we have seen, ordinary, respectable Germans, who had worked hard all their lives, lost out, whilst debtors and big business did well. This turned many people against the government.

It was hard to have confidence in the government when everything was in such chaos. Some of the government's other problems had been outside their control but hyper-inflation was caused by the government's own actions. This made many moderate people turn against the Weimar Republic.

In future years few people in Germany would forget the damage caused by hyper-inflation. Some historians have claimed that it damaged the Weimar Republic more than any other event in the first five years of its existence. What do you think?

Activity

Look at the five problems the Weimar Republic faced between 1918 and 1923:

- **DEFEAT IN THE FIRST WORLD WAR – THE 'STAB IN THE BACK'**

- **THE TREATY OF VERSAILLES**

- **POLITICAL VIOLENCE**

- **INVASION OF THE RUHR**

- **HYPER-INFLATION**

Rank these in order, starting with the problem that you think damaged the Weimar Republic the most, and ending with the one that you think damaged it the least. Explain each decision you make.

How were the problems faced by the Weimar Republic linked together?

Activity

Look at the picture below. Five students are working together to find links between the different problems faced by the Weimar Republic. One link has been explained for you.

1   On your own version of this diagram, in bubble 2 explain how the Treaty of Versailles is linked to Political Violence. In bubble 3 explain how the Treaty is linked to the Invasion of the Ruhr.

2   Can you find any other links between other problems? Make sure that you can explain the links.

3   Which problem do you think was at the root of the difficulties facing the Weimar Republic? Look for the problem that is linked to the most other problems.

HYPER-INFLATION

DEFEAT IN THE FIRST WORLD WAR – THE 'STAB IN THE BACK'

THE TREATY OF VERSAILLES

3

2

INVASION OF THE RUHR

POLITICAL VIOLENCE

1 As a result of the invasion of the Ruhr the government lost income from one of the most important industrial areas. They became very short of money. The government responded by printing more money and this led to hyper-inflation.

smarter revision

Most events in History have several causes or results. You could use an activity like the one above to explore links between factors in other events in this depth study.

By now you should feel like an expert on the Weimar Republic in the early 1920s! However, simply knowing a lot is not enough to achieve a good grade in the GCSE exam. Exam Busters are ready to help you.

Look at the exam question below.

> **Describe** the problems the Weimar Republic faced in the early 1920s.
>
> [9]

You will get questions like this as the first part of Question 5 or 6 on your paper: 5a or 6a.

You can see that it worth 9 marks, so it is quite an important question: give it about 13 minutes.

But it looks pretty straightforward, doesn't it? The temptation is just to list all the problems that the Weimar Republic faced. But a good 'describe' answer needs more than that.

What makes a good answer to this question?

- A list of the problems is not good enough. Do not just say that hyper-inflation was a problem, prove it was! Provide supporting evidence to back up each point that you make.

- Select and use information carefully. Do not include everything you know about the Weimar Republic in your answer. Choose information that is relevant to the question and use it in the right place.

What makes an excellent answer?

- Don't be satisfied with just giving a couple of problems. Examine a range of problems. You should have time to cover four or five problems.

- Make sure your answer is well-organised. It is important that you plan your answer before you start to write it. Use paragraphs! In this case each paragraph should deal with one problem.

Linking factors

The Weimar Republic faced many problems in the early 1920s. One problem was that it was set up at a very difficult time. Germany faced defeat in the First World War and the new government had little choice but to sign an armistice. The German people hated the leaders of the new republic for signing this.* A second problem was the Treaty of Versailles, which followed the armistice. It was very harsh on Germany. Lots of land was taken away and Germany had to pay massive reparations.**

In 1923 things got even worse for the Weimar Republic. The French invaded the Ruhr and there was hyper-inflation. Also, there was political violence. In 1923 the Nazis attempted a putsch in Munich. The Weimar Republic therefore faced lots of problems.

* A good opening but the student needs to explain why many Germans were angered by the new government's decision to sign the armistice. The student needs to explain that many Germans believed that they had been 'stabbed in the back'.

** The student could have provided more specific information to support this argument. For example, '13 per cent of Germany's land was taken away'. Also, the Treaty of Versailles could be linked to other problems. Using phrases such as 'this meant that…' or 'this led to…' the student should aim to explain how the Treaty of Versailles created serious problems.

Activities

1 Look at the answer above. To the right are the examiner's comments on the first paragraph. Imagine that you are an examiner. Explain to the student how they could improve the rest of their answer.

2 Now write your own answer to the exam question. Swap your work with a partner. Once again imagine you are an examiner. Highlight anything that you think could be improved upon and explain how it could be improved.

For your GCSE exam you need to develop your recall skills. It is no good going into the exam knowing how to structure a good answer if you cannot remember any important information!

How do you normally revise? You probably make revision notes or simply read through your folder. Throughout this book you will be provided with some different strategies. Experiment and find out which method works best for you.

SMARTER REVISION can save you time and improve your grades!

Acronyms

Acronyms are a really useful way of remembering several linked items – several causes, results, aspects of a topic. You could compete with your friends to make up good acronyms as you go through this course.

How can a lamb help you to remember the terms of the Treaty of Versailles?

Revision does not have to be boring! Inventing your own acronyms can help you remember key pieces of information. The odder it is, the more likely you are to remember it.

Take, for example, the Treaty of Versailles. You need to remember the four key terms of the Treaty. Think of the Germans being like LAMBs to the slaughter. A LAMB can help you to remember the key terms.

L = **Land** (Germany lost 13 per cent of its land.)

A = **Army** (The German army was cut to just 100,000.)

M = **Money** (Germany was made to pay reparations.)

B = **Blame** (Germany was blamed for starting the war.

Activity

Invent an acronym to help you remember the five problems faced by the Weimar Republic (see page 16).

How can a map save you time and boost your memory?

- Memory maps encourage you to link pieces of information together. You learn more by making links, because it makes you think! You are actively involved with your revision. This is a lot better than simply reading through your folder hoping that your brain will act as a sponge and soak up the information!

- You remember even better if you add your own images.

- Memory maps can be added to over time and built up over a module or unit of work. They are also a flexible tool for revision. You can produce a memory map from memory, check it against the original, then add in what you have missed.

- Finally, and perhaps most importantly, memory maps make revision a lot more interesting!

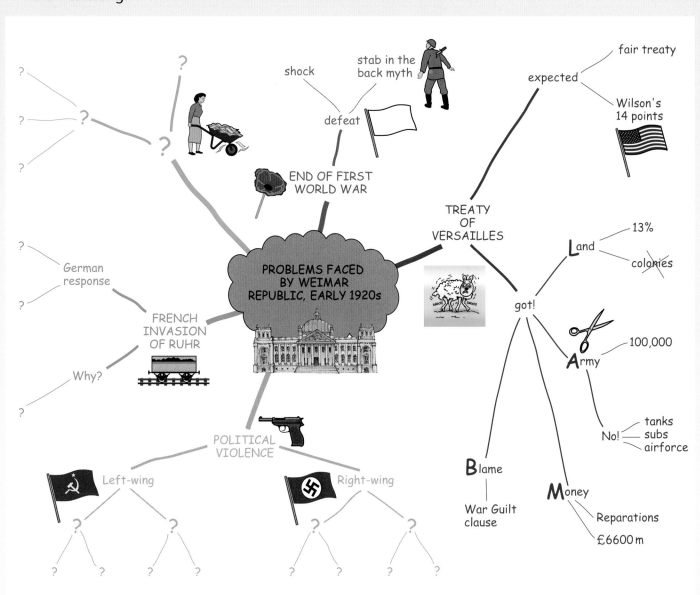

How to build a memory map

Step 1 Use plain A4 or, even better, A3 paper. Space is important. The end result should not look too busy or cramped. Using the paper landscape usually works better.

Step 2 Draw the first draft of your map in pencil so that you can make any corrections that are needed.

Step 3 Draw a central picture which sums up the topic for you. Start in the middle . . . then build out . . .

Step 4 Divide the topic into sub-topics – what are the main ideas in the topic? Work in a clockwise direction (starting at 2 o'clock). Draw a line out from the central image (this is like the large bough of a tree) for each theme/sub-topic. Write the theme/sub-topic on the bough. If possible, each theme should be in a different colour.

Step 5 Draw branches off the main bough using the same colour. On each branch write down key words connected to the theme or sub-topic. Write these slightly smaller than the main theme.

Step 6 You can now sub-divide again. Draw thinner lines off the branches (twigs if you like) to record any ideas that are connected to the words on each branch. You can continue sub-dividing, depending on the amount of detail you wish to include. As you move further away from the centre, the ideas become less important (central) to the main topic. This is reflected by decreasing the size of the words and images as you move away from the centre.

- Do not write full sentences. Be ruthless! **Use key words** or phrases. This makes it easier to build up branches without using the whole page. You can't write down everything you know about a topic, and you don't need to! Ninety per cent of the words that students write down when they make revision notes are not needed for recall purposes!
- **Use pictures/images/diagrams** as often as you can, to replace words or to emphasise words. Remember, lots of you will find it easier to remember visual images than words.
- **PRINT** words to make them stand out.
- Include **acronyms** where possible. Remember, the odder the better!
- Add to or **redraft** your map when you do later work that revisits or builds on the ideas in the map. So remember to leave some space!

Activity

Use the advice on pages 20–21 to complete the memory map opposite. You can use your own images if you wish.

1.2 Was the Weimar Republic ever a success?

The story of the Weimar Republic is not all doom. For five 'Golden Years', 1924–1929, things appeared to go well in Germany. But you must judge for yourself if the old problems had really been dealt with, or just papered over.

Problems faced by the Weimar Republic

POLICY A
Print even more money. Use it to pay the workers on strike in the Ruhr and to pay compensation to people who have lost their savings.

PROBLEM 1
Hyper-inflation

POLICY B
Scrap the old money system and set up a new currency.

POLICY A
Call off passive resistance. Promise to begin paying reparations again to France to persuade them to leave.

PROBLEM 2
French occupation of the Ruhr

POLICY B
Continue passive resistance. Pay the workers in the Ruhr so that they can continue their strike. Threaten to force the French to leave if they won't go willingly.

POLICY A
Threaten war unless you are given back the land you lost in the Treaty of Versailles. Secretly start building up your army.

PROBLEM 3
Germany is not trusted by other countries

POLICY B
Make a series of treaties with other European countries. Promise to stick to the terms of the Treaty of Versailles and not to try to regain the land you lost.

POLICY A
Refuse to pay the Allies any more money. Argue that the terms of the Treaty of Versailles are unfair and that it is impossible to keep up with reparations payments.

PROBLEM 4
Germany is facing massive reparations

POLICY B
Promise to stick to the terms of the Treaty and pay reparations in full. Try and persuade the Allies to let you have longer to pay back the money you owe. Borrow money from the rich USA so that you can start paying back reparations immediately.

POLICY A
Try to get loans from the rich USA. Use this money to build new homes, roads and hospitals. Tax rich people more and use the money to increase pensions and help the unemployed.

PROBLEM 5
Germany needs to rebuild its economy

POLICY B
Refuse to ask for foreign loans. Argue that it is humiliating and that Germany should not be dependent on other countries. Provide jobs for the unemployed by building up the army. Instead of paying reparations use the money to build homes and roads.

To what extent did Stresemann solve the problems facing the Weimar Republic?

In August 1923 Gustav Stresemann became Chancellor of Germany. The problems he faced were so great most Germans did not think that he or any of the politicians of the Weimar Republic would be able to solve them.

For the next five years (first as Chancellor, then as Foreign Minister) Stresemann tried to find answers to the problems facing the Weimar Republic. How far he succeeded is a debate among historians. It is time for you to join the debate!

HISTORIAN A SAYS: 'Stresemann – the man who built a strong Germany'

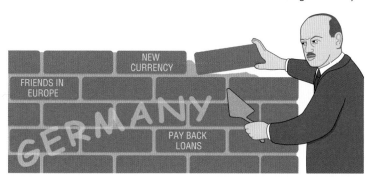

Stresemann was one of Germany's greatest leaders. He came up with clever solutions to the problems that Germany faced in 1923 and built a strong Germany. By the time he died in 1929, Germany had one of the strongest economies in Europe. It was trusted and well respected by other countries. So the period 1924–1929 is rightly called the 'Golden Twenties'.

HISTORIAN B SAYS: 'Stresemann – the man who papered over the cracks'

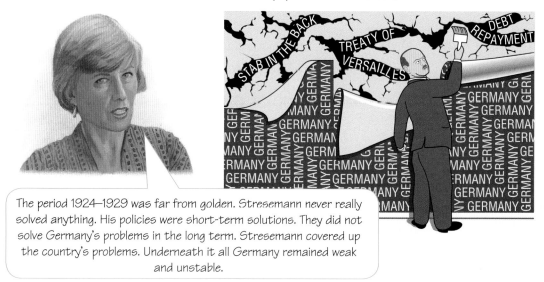

The period 1924–1929 was far from golden. Stresemann never really solved anything. His policies were short-term solutions. They did not solve Germany's problems in the long term. Stresemann covered up the country's problems. Underneath it all Germany remained weak and unstable.

When it comes to revision time, students sometimes revise randomly: they simply learn as much as they can about all sorts of things, then try to regurgitate it all in the exam. As a result, one of the most common criticisms that examiners make of candidates' answers is that students simply list 'everything they know about a topic' rather than selecting relevant information to support their answer or their viewpoint.

Charts help you overcome this problem because they make you think about the content, and help you to organise the information at the point you learn it, so you can use it in a logical way. For example, the chart on this page asks you to record the key details of Stresemann's policies. It then asks you to analyse the positive and negative results of the policies. This is just the kind of thing you may be asked to do in an exam. So when the examiner asks you a question about the recovery of the Weimar republic in the period 1924–1929, the work you did to make this chart means you are ready for the question. The information you need is there in your chart (and, if you revise it, in your mind) already. Your chart helps you to write relevantly on the subject.

Through the book you will make a number of charts like this (on pages 52, 64 and 75). So fill in each chart carefully and keep it for revision time.

Activity

1   Use pages 24–25 to fill in your own copy of the table below. In the last column give Stresemann a star rating to show how successful each policy was. (***** 5 brilliant solution; * 1 very poor solution.)

Problem	Stresemann's policy	Positive results	Negative results	Star rating
Hyper-inflation				
French occupation of the Ruhr				
Germany is not trusted by other countries				
Germany is facing massive reparations				
Germany needs to rebuild its economy				

2   Look for similarities and differences between what Stresemann did and what you chose on page 22. Do you think that Stresemann made mistakes, or did he have no other option?

Stresemann's solutions

POLICY 1: Introduce a new currency

- Stresemann acted quickly to deal with hyper-inflation. The old money was replaced with a new currency called the Rentenmark. One Rentenmark replaced 1000 billion marks. Old notes were recalled and burned.

Result...
- The new currency was quickly accepted by the German people. Inflation was brought under control.

However...
- The German people never forgot hyper-inflation. People who had lost their savings were not compensated. They felt cheated and they blamed the Weimar Republic.

POLICY 2: Persuade the French to leave the Ruhr

- Stresemann called off passive resistance, because it had not forced the French to withdraw from the Ruhr and it had created serious economic problems.
- He promised to keep up reparation payments to France.

Result...
- The French left the Ruhr.

However...
- This was a very unpopular policy in Germany. There was a lot of opposition to it, especially from right-wing extremists. They claimed that it was a sign of weak government. Stresemann had 'given in' to the French.

POLICY 3: Improve Germany's relationships with other countries

- He decided to co-operate with other countries in Europe. He accepted that Germany could not reclaim the land it had lost in the Treaty of Versailles. He hoped that by doing so the Allies would change the terms of the Treaty.

Result...

- In 1925 Stresemann signed the Locarno Pacts. These were a series of treaties with Britain, France, Belgium and Italy in which they promised not to invade one another.
- In 1926 Germany joined the League of Nations. It was given 'great power' status which meant that it could have a say in major decisions that had to be made.
- In 1926 Stresemann was awarded the Nobel Peace Prize.

However...

- Some Germans thought that Stresemann was weak. By saying that Germany would not try to regain the land it had lost he had once again 'given in' to France.
- Some army generals believed that Stresemann should have built up the army instead and tried to regain the land lost in the Treaty of Versailles, by force.

POLICY 4: Continue to pay reparations

- Stresemann realised that he could not force the Allies to change the Treaty so he promised to pay reparations. He hoped that the Allies would lower the payments in the future.

Result...

- The Dawes Plan of 1924, reorganised the way that Germans had to pay reparations. Germany was given a longer period to pay the Allies.
- In 1929 the Young Plan lowered the amount of money Germany had to pay in reparations from 132,000 million marks to 37,000 million.

However...

- The Dawes Plan did not reduce the amount of money Germany had to pay in reparations. Opponents of the Weimar Republic called the Dawes Plan 'a second Versailles'.
- The Young Plan was also hated by many Germans who thought that Germany should not have to pay reparations at all. Under the terms of the Young Plan, Germany would be paying reparations until 1988.

POLICY 5: Get help to rebuild the economy

- Stresemann organised big loans for Germany from the USA. This was part of the Dawes Plan (1924).

Result...

- The German government used this money to improve housing, hospitals, schools and roads.
- Loans were also given to private German firms.
- In addition, many US firms set up factories in Germany.
- Pensions and wages rose (for some).

However...

- The German economy was now very dependent on the US economy. Problems in the USA would cause massive problems in Germany. Even Stresemann himself admitted that Germany was 'dancing on a volcano'.
- Wages did not rise for everyone. Farmers lost out because food prices stayed low. By 1929 farmworkers earned only half the national average wage. Many farmers became angry and started to support extreme groups, such as the Nazis, who offered to help them.
- Unemployment never fell below 1 million. From 1928 it started to rise even higher.
- Rich people in Germany had to pay higher taxes. They complained that the government was spending too much money on helping the poor and the unemployed.

And one more thing...

After 1923 Germany became more peaceful. There was less political violence. Between 1924 and 1928 there were no attempts to overthrow the Weimar Republic.

GCSE history is not all about writing essays. You also need to be able to use visual sources, like cartoons and photographs, effectively. This page helps you with cartoons. Here is a sample exam question.

Give **two** things you can learn from Source 1 about Stresemann and Weimar Germany.   [4]

Source A

flowers   Stresemann

tightrope

ravine

◀ A cartoon from *Simplicissimus*, a German political magazine, 1923

Germany is represented as a child. This suggests that it was young and needed lots of guidance. Stresemann is shown as preventing Germany falling into the ravine.

You will meet a question on sources, worded something like this one, as the first question on your exam paper, Question 1.

You can see that it only worth 4 marks, the lowest-scoring question on the paper, so don't spend too long on it: 6 minutes is enough. However, the trick is to make sure you don't drop easy marks here, but score all four!

To get all four marks you must do more than just describe what you can see in the source – you must also explain it. Cartoons and posters usually contain a very strong message. Try to work out, or **infer**, what this message is. An *inference* is something you can get from a source but which isn't stated in so many words, or obvious from a picture.

Use all the clues in the source. A lot of time and thought goes into designing cartoons. Every feature gives you a clue about the message. You could label all the people and objects in the source (as we have begun to do for Source A). Then ask yourself the key question: why has the artist included these details in the cartoon?

For example, in Source A:

• Why is Germany walking on a tightrope?
• Why is Germany crossing a ravine?
• Why are there flowers on the other side?
• Why is Stresemann an angel?

Once you have worked out what you can *infer* from the cartoon, be sure to use what you can see in your answer.

An *unsupported inference* is where you don't use anything from the source to explain why you've made that inference; it will get you 2 out of 4 marks.

A *supported inference* is where you back up what you have got from the source by making a specific reference to something in it. For example, the second sentence above, suggesting why Germany is shown as a child, is a *supported inference*.

Look at this question.

'Stresemann was successful in overcoming many of Germany's problems.' Do you agree? Explain your answer. [16]

This type of exam question comes right at the end of your paper, the second part of Question 5 or 6 – 5b or 6b. You will have seen at once that it is worth 16 marks. This is the highest scoring question on the paper, so you should make sure you leave plenty of time for it: you should find you have 25 minutes.

This high-scoring question tests your knowledge of Stresemann and your ability to write a balanced account. Follow the steps below to help you write a high level answer.

Step 1 **The argument for**
Look back at the historians' arguments on page 23. What evidence would you use to support the claim of Historian A?
Look back at the table you produced on page 24. Select five pieces of evidence to support the argument that Stresemann solved many of the problems facing the Weimar Republic. **Selection** is important. In the exam you will not have time to write down everything that Stresemann did.
You should have enough evidence here to write a good first paragraph.

Step 2 **The argument against**
What evidence could you use to support the claim of Historian B? Select evidence from your table to support the argument that Stresemann failed to solve the really important problems facing the Weimar Republic.
This will form the basis of your second paragraph.

Step 3 **The conclusion**
Producing a balanced answer does not mean that you can opt out of a conclusion or simply say that Stresemann solved some of the problems, but not others. Sitting on the fence is a dangerous position. Your answer collapses and you lose marks!
Instead, be confident and **reach an overall judgement**. Weigh the two arguments. Which historian would you side with in a debate? Who has the strongest evidence to support their claim? Write down your opinion and explain why you have come to this conclusion.

Remember, writing a balanced account is difficult. We will return to ways of dealing with this question later in this section, on page 45, and in Section 2, on page 62.

1.3 Why had the Nazi Party achieved so little by 1928?

Now we must go back to the end of the First World War to find out about Hitler and the Nazis. You will find out what they were saying and doing, and how they gained supporters. You must explain who was attracted to the Nazi message and why support for the Party did not amount to much by 1928.

In Section 1.1 you investigated four groups that tried to overthrow the Weimar Republic. One of these groups was the Nazi Party. In 1923 they tried to take over Germany by force. They failed, and their leader, Adolf Hitler, was sent to prison. However, this was not the end of the Nazi Party, nor was it the last the German people would hear of Adolf Hiter. Look back to the report that you wrote on the Nazi party, for the Activity on page 11. It will help you with your next big task.

Activity

December, 1928

Dear Secret Agent

TOP SECRET

We were very impressed with the report that you wrote for the German Government about the different groups that planned to overthrow the Weimar Republic. We would like to use your expertise again.

We are still interested in the activities of the Nazi Party. Since his release from prison, their leader, Adolf Hitler, has been working very hard to rebuild the Nazi Party. Your task is to find out as much as you can about Hitler, the Nazi Party and its supporters. What do they really stand for? Are they well organised? Are they more dangerous now than they were in 1923?

This time we would like you to present your findings to us in person. All the leading members of the government will be present, so you need to plan your presentation carefully. We have put together four Evidence Files to help you with your research (see pages 29–32). We suggest that you organise your presentation under the following headings:

Section 1: Leadership – Who is Adolf Hitler? What is his background? Is he an effective leader?

Section 2: Beliefs – What does the Nazi Party stand for? What are their big ideas?

Section 3: Organisation – Is the Nazi Party well organised?

Section 4: Support – Who supports the Nazi Party? How much support does it have?

Section 5: Danger rating – Do you think that the Nazi Party has grown more dangerous since 1923?

(Use a danger rating scale: !!!!! = very dangerous; ! = no threat at all. Does it look as if they will get into power soon?)

FILE 1: LEADER PROFILE – ADOLF HITLER

Early life
- Born in 1889 in Austria.
- Unhappy at school. He is moody, shy and lonely.
- Poor at most subjects (except gym and art).
- 1903 – Father dies.
- Leaves school with no qualifications.

Life after school
- 1907 – Mother dies. Goes to Vienna. Fails to gain a place at Academy of Fine Arts. Struggles to make money and lives almost as a down-and-out.
- 1914 – Joins the German army. Fights in the First World War, winning a medal for bravery.
- 1918 – Angry to hear of Germany's surrender. Feels betrayed.

Political life

- 1919 – Employed as a spy by the army. Sent to a meeting of the German Workers' Party. Finds himself agreeing with many of their ideas. Joins as their 55th member.
- 1920 – Helps to write their political programme (see File 2). The Party is renamed the National Socialist German Workers' Party (or Nazi Party).
- 1921 – Hitler becomes leader of the Nazi Party. He sets up the SA (see File 3), the Nazi Party's private army.
- Support for the Nazi Party grows. By the end of 1922 it has 20,000 members.
- 1923 – The Munich Putsch. The Nazis attempt to overthrow the government by force. The putsch fails but the trial and publicity that follow give Hitler the chance to make a name for himself.
- 1924 – In prison, he writes *Mein Kampf* (My Struggle). This book outlines his main ideas about how Germany should be ruled (see File 2).
- Hitler is released from prison early. He starts to rebuild the Nazi Party, improving the way it is organised and changing its tactics (see File 3). His aim now is to use democratic means, rather than force, to get into power.

Leadership qualities
- Tremendous energy
- Charismatic and inspirational
- Single-minded and suspicious of others
- Great public speaker. His timing, the style of his delivery and the content of his speeches captivate his listeners.

FILE 2: BELIEFS

The Programme (aims) of the National Socialist German Workers' Party, 1920

- Destroy the Treaty of Versailles and end reparations.
- Only those of German blood may be members of the nation (Germany). Therefore no Jew may be a member of the nation.
- All non-German immigration to be stopped.
- Take over land in Eastern Europe in order to provide 'living space' for the growing German population.
- Criminals against the nation should be punished by death.
- Provide generous old age pensions.
- Abolish incomes not earned by work.
- Help should be given to small businesses.
- Change the education system. Pupils should be taught to love their country. Physical fitness should be encouraged. Sport and gymnastics must be compulsory.

F
I
L
E

2

Extracts from *Mein Kampf*, 1924

One strong leader. Debate and discussion produce weak government. There should be no majority decisions. Instead of democracy, decisions should be taken by one man.

Smash Communism.

The Aryans (white Europeans) are the Master Race. All other races (especially the Jews) are inferior.

Unite all Germans in one country.

Rebuild the army and invade land in Eastern Europe. Armed struggle is an essential part of life.

FILE 3: ORGANISATION AND TACTICS

Report on Nazi Party tactics, 1928

The Nazis appear to have changed their tactics. Hitler seems to have realised that they cannot seize power by force. He is trying to build up support for the Nazi Party so that they can take power by democratic means. Since Hitler's release from prison he has reorganised the Nazi Party to make it more electable.

- The Nazis have been running evening classes for their members in order to make them better public speakers.
- Local leaders of the Nazi Party have been organising public meetings, with visiting speakers, in an attempt to gain more supporters.
- The Nazis receive most of their money from ordinary members, through donations and charges to attend meetings.
- Their propaganda is very effective and they concentrate on issues that people think are important.
- They have adopted the raised right arm as a salute and the swastika as their symbol. Hitler himself has designed their flag.

Report on the SA, 1928

SA stands for 'Stürm-Abteilung', or Stormtroopers. The SA are sometimes known as 'Brownshirts' because of the colour of their uniform. More than half of the members come from the unemployed and many are ex-soldiers who fought in the First World War. The SA provide them with food and sometimes a home in SA-run hostels.

The SA are growing increasingly powerful. Hitler set up the SA in 1921 to stop Nazi meetings being interrupted by followers of other parties. However, now the SA are far more likely to disrupt the meetings of their opponents. Hitler uses them like a bunch of hired thugs. Their aim is to use any means possible to stop opponents of the Nazi Party spreading their message. Hitler has said, 'We must struggle with ideas, but if necessary also with fists.'

The SA are very important to Hitler. They protect Nazi speakers and help to deliver propaganda leaflets to people's homes. Some Germans are put off by their violence but others seem to be impressed by their organisation.

F
I
L
E

3

FILE 4: SUPPORT

Report on the 1928 election

The Nazis must be very disappointed with the result of the 1928 election. The great majority of workers supported the Social Democrats. With the help of foreign loans, Stresemann has got the economy back on track. Many factory workers feel that they are doing quite well at the moment. Those workers who do want major changes seem to be voting for the Communist Party. In the last election the Communists gained four times as many votes as the Nazis. Hitler does not appear to be getting his message across to workers.

The Nazis have been more successful with farmers and the owners of small businesses. These groups have not done so well recently and are starting to turn to the Nazis.

More people are members of the Nazi Party than ever before. Membership has almost doubled between 1923 and 1928. However, the vast majority of Germans do not appear to be attracted to the Nazi Party. After all, the Nazis got under 3 per cent of the overall votes in the election.

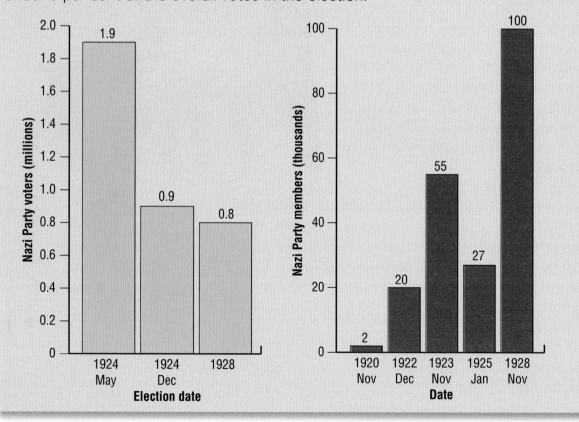

F
I
L
E

4

Who did the Nazis appeal to in 1928?

Dietrich

I was proud to fight for Germany in the First World War. The army was stabbed in the back by the criminals who signed the peace treaty. I loved army life – the uniform, the friendship, the excitement. During the war my life had a purpose. Now I just work in a factory. This country needs strong leadership, like we had in the army. With a strong leader our country could become great again.

Josef

I'm a Jewish businessman. I also fought for Germany in the First World War. The Treaty of Versailles was a disgrace. Our government should never have given in to the Allies. During the early 1920s I lost a lot of my savings because of hyper-inflation. However, Stresemann seems to have sorted things out and my business is doing well. I hope it continues.

Maria

I am a 20-year-old student and an active member of the Communist Party. I think the Government should be doing more to help the workers. All the money goes to the handful of rich industrialists who own the factories. Things need to change.

Franz

Helga

My husband's factory is doing very well at the moment. Stresemann has done a great job. The US loans have been a real boost. Business is booming. I'm also pleased that all the political violence has stopped. There is no place for violence in a civilised country. The only thing that scares me is the Communists. It would be a disaster if they took over the country. The last thing we want is for Germany to go the same way as the Soviet Union.

I am a farm worker. The farmer I work for has had to cut my wages. I don't blame him, I blame the Government. Farmers are losing out because of low food prices and the politicians don't seem to care. I'm also worried about my parents. They are both pensioners. They lost a lot of money during the hyper-inflation a few years ago. They have worked hard all their life but they are struggling to survive on what they receive from the Government.

1 Look at the people here. Who would be most likely to vote for the Nazi Party? Explain your answer.

2 Work in pairs. Imagine that the five people are being interviewed for a German radio programme in 1928. The radio reporter is trying to find out how each person feels about the Nazis. The reporter wants to ask them:
   a) Which of the Nazis' policies (beliefs/ideas) do they like? Which do they dislike?
   b) Would they consider voting for the Nazis? What are their main reasons for this?

Take it in turns to play the role of interviewer and interviewee. You could record each interview on tape or perform an interview in front of the rest of your class.

Why had the Nazis failed to get into power by 1928?

The 1928 election showed that the Nazi Party was a long way from getting into power. Less than 3 per cent of Germans had voted for the Nazis. As Hitler approached his fortieth birthday his dream of ruling Germany appeared to be fading. Why was this the case, when he had put so much work into reorganising the Nazi Party?

Explanation 1: The Nazis lacked the support of the working class

- Most workers voted for the Social Democratic Party.
- Workers who wanted to see change tended to vote for the Communist Party rather than the Nazis.

How the working classes voted

Explanation 2: 1924–1929 was a time of peace and prosperity

- Stresemann had managed to solve many of the economic problems of the early 1920s. Loans from foreign countries had helped to rebuild the German economy. As a result, most people felt better off.
- Stresemann had built better relationships with other countries and political violence inside Germany had decreased.

Explanation 3: The Nazis' ideas were too extreme

- People were put off by the Nazis' anti-semitic ideas and their aim of invading other countries.
- The SA were very violent. They were seen by many people as little more than hired thugs.

Discuss

1 Are any of Explanations 1–3 linked?
2 Which explanation do you think is the most significant? (You may want to consider why you thought some of the people on page 33 would not have voted for the Nazis.)

Look at this question.

> Why had the Nazis not got into power by 1928? [12]
>
> You may use the following in your answer and any other ideas of your own:
> - 1923 rentenmark issued
> - 1924 Hitler released from prison
> - 1924–1929 German economic recovery

You will find a question worded like this as Question 3 or Question 4 of your examination paper. You can see that it is worth 12 marks, which is quite a lot: give it nearly 20 minutes.

You can also see that the examiner provides three bullet-points to prompt you with things you could write about. We'll show you how to deal with these later in this book, on page 45. For now, we'll concentrate on making sure you answer the question.

- As you can see, this is a **why** question: you have to **explain** why the Nazis had failed to win power by 1928. Don't write down everything you know about the Nazi Party in the 1920s.
- Decide on **three key reasons** why they had failed to win power.
- Provide specific information to support your key arguments.

During the 1920s the Nazis had worked hard to build up support but in the 1928 election the Nazis only gained 3 per cent of the vote. When he was in prison Hitler wrote down his ideas in his book Mein Kampf. After he came out of prison he reorganised the Party. Nazi Party members went to evening classes where they were trained in public speaking. The Nazis also improved their propaganda but they did not increase the number of people who voted for them.

One reason was that they did not manage to persuade working-class people to vote for them. Most of the working class voted for the Social Democratic Party. Those workers who wanted change tended to vote for the Communist Party.

The Communists wanted to totally change Germany and make it like the Soviet Union. The Soviet Union had been taken over by the Communists during the First World War.

The Nazis also managed to put some people off voting for them. Many people thought that the Nazis' anti-Jewish ideas were too extreme and that the SA was too violent. The SA was sometimes known as the 'brownshirts' because of the colour of their uniform.

Another reason that made it difficult for the Nazis was that Stresemann had managed to improve the German economy. In 1924 he organised the Dawes Plan. This means that Germany got large sums of money from the USA which they used to build new factories. However, the loans made Germany very dependent on the USA. Some Germans did not like this, but many people in Germany were happy with the changes Stresemann had made.

Activity

Read the answer below. This student has clearly written a lot, but it doesn't answer the WHY question. Your task is to improve it.

1. Look at each paragraph in turn. In each of these paragraphs the student goes off the point. Decide which sentences are irrelevant to answering the WHY question and could be CUT.

2. Where the student has provided some good information, add a sentence making clear how the information helps to explain why the Nazis had not won power by 1928.

1.4 How did Hitler become Chancellor in 1933?

In 1928 few Germans would have predicted that Hitler would become leader of Germany. The Nazi Party did not appear to be going anywhere. Yet by July 1932 the Nazis were the most popular party, and in January 1933 Hitler became Chancellor. You need to identify the key reasons behind Hitler's dramatic rise to power.

In this section two teams of historians are going to try and persuade you that they have the strongest explanation. You need to think carefully and make your own decision.

Which team of historians are you going to support in the tug-of-war?

We believe that the Nazis got into power because of **their own actions**. Effective leadership, clever promises, good organisation and brilliant propaganda are the main reasons Hitler gained power.

Activity

Step 1 – Evidence collection
On pages 38–43 each team member puts forward an argument to support their team's overall case. Record their argument and any evidence that they use to support it. You could use a memory map or a table to help you record your findings.

Step 2 – Weigh the evidence that you have collected
How strong is the argument put forward by each team member? Give each team member a rating out of 10 to show how important you think their argument is.
Then ask yourself the key question – which team do you think has the strongest overall argument?

Step 3 – Present your case
Write a speech supporting the team you think has the strongest argument. Aim to use written sources, graphs, statistics and photographs to support your case.
Be prepared to take part in a debate with the rest of your class. You may find that some of them disagree with you!

My team disagree! We believe that the Nazis were helped by **events they had no control over**. The Wall Street Crash, fear of Communism, weak opponents and a political deal are the key factors that explain how Hitler got into power.

OTHER EVENTS

I believe that the key event in Hitler's rise to power was the Wall Street Crash. This led to a terrible economic crisis in Germany. This crisis was known as the Great Depression and it explains why many people started to vote for extreme parties like the Nazis.

THE WALL STREET CRASH

Why did events in the USA cause problems in Germany?

When the US stockmarket on Wall Street crashed, in 1929, it created many problems. People lost the confidence to invest in companies and US banks and businesses lost large sums of money. As a result, one in four people became unemployed.

This created serious problems for countries in Europe that traded with the USA. Germany was particularly badly hit. The whole German economy was very dependent on loans from America. As can be seen in the diagram below, a vicious circle was created causing unemployment and widespread poverty. This period in German history is known as the Great Depression.

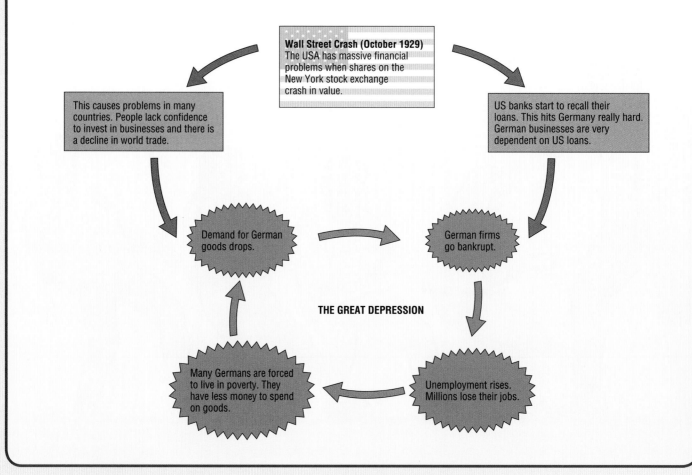

Wall Street Crash (October 1929)
The USA has massive financial problems when shares on the New York stock exchange crash in value.

This causes problems in many countries. People lack confidence to invest in businesses and there is a decline in world trade.

US banks start to recall their loans. This hits Germany really hard. German businesses are very dependent on US loans.

Demand for German goods drops.

German firms go bankrupt.

THE GREAT DEPRESSION

Many Germans are forced to live in poverty. They have less money to spend on goods.

Unemployment rises. Millions lose their jobs.

The Great Depression had three main effects.

1 The Depression made life a great struggle for people

The effects of the Great Depression were felt throughout Germany. Many businesses went bankrupt. Those that survived saw their profits drop. Farmers also struggled and many went out of business. By 1932 unemployment had reached 6 million.

2 People thought the government was not doing enough to help

- The government found it difficult to agree on how to respond to the Great Depression. For a long time they did very little to help people in need.
- The government was worried about spending extra money to help people hit by unemployment and poverty. They thought that spending more money could lead to hyper-inflation.
- As more people lost their jobs the government received less money from taxes. They responded by cutting back the amount of money that they spent to help those in need. This made the government even more unpopular.

THIS LED TO…

3 The Depression increased support for extreme parties

- The Great Depression made people angry. Many blamed the political parties that had been running the country and the democratic way that the Weimar Republic was governed. The depression made the government look weak and powerless. People started to turn to more extreme political parties instead.
- The unemployment and poverty caused by the Great Depression had a significant impact on how Germans voted. The graphs below show that as unemployment increased so did the support for more extreme political parties.

Source 1

Unemployment figures and votes for the Nazis and the Communists in Reichstag elections, 1928–1932

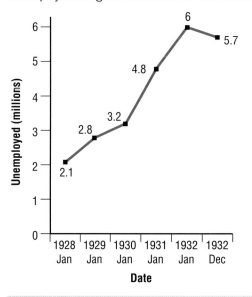

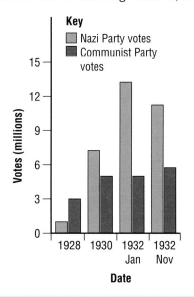

OWN ACTIONS

Hold on! It's about time you heard from some of my team. We admit that events such as the Wall Street Crash helped the Nazis but we do not believe that this is the **main** reason that they were able to get into power. If you really want to understand how Hitler got into power you need to look at what the Nazis were doing **themselves**.

A — HITLER'S LEADERSHIP SKILLS

Hitler's leadership skills played a crucial role in the Nazis' rise to power. His speeches and personality gained the Nazis a great deal of support. He came across as a strong leader who could solve Germany's problems.

HITLER'S LEADERSHIP

Hitler was a strong leader who was able to make people believe that he alone could save them from the problems facing Germany. He was also a very charismatic and powerful public speaker. He seemed to be able to identify with his audience and to fill them with a sense of hope.

Source 2

Adapted from *Darkness over Germany*, 1943, by E. A. Butler

As Hitler spoke I was most interested to hear the reactions of the men around me. 'He speaks for me, he speaks for me.' 'Oh God, he knows how I feel.' Many of them seemed lost to the world around them and were probably unaware of what they were saying. One man in particular struck me as he lent forward with his head in his hands, and with a sort of sob said, 'God be thanked, he understands.'

B — NAZI PROMISES

Nazi promises.
The Nazis said what people wanted to hear. They made sure that their promises were flexible and contained something for everyone. This explains why they were so well supported.

PROMISES

The Nazis concentrated on issues that the German people were very unhappy about. They promised to
- solve Germany's economic problems
- provide strong leadership
- ignore the Treaty of Versailles
- build up the army and
- make Germany a great country again.

Their promises were designed to appeal to everyone, from businessmen and farmers to factory workers and housewives. The Nazis were very flexible in what they said to the German people. If they found that a policy was unpopular they would simply drop it.

C

ORGANISATION

Organisation.
The Nazis were also very well organised. This impressed voters and helped the Nazis to campaign more effectively than their main rivals.

The Nazis were able to raise money to fund their election campaigns. A lot of this money came from ordinary members. The Nazis were also able to attract huge donations from rich businessmen like Fritz Thyssen.

Nazi party members worked hard in their local regions to spread the Nazi message through door-to-door leafleting and public meetings. Nazi posters could be seen everywhere. The Nazis also organised soup kitchens and shelters for the unemployed.

The SA also played an important role. These were violent times. People liked the fact that the SA were prepared to stand up to the Communists who often fought battles with the police. With their uniforms and marches the SA looked capable of bringing law and order to Germany.

Source 3

Inside the Third Reich by Albert Speer
… during these months my mother saw an SA parade in the streets. The sight of discipline in a time of chaos, the impression of energy in a time of hopelessness, seems to have won her over. Without ever having heard a speech or read a pamphlet, she joined the party.

D

NAZI PROPAGANDA

Nazi propaganda was the main reason why support for the Nazis grew. It presented the Nazi Party as the solution to Germany's problems.

Nazi propaganda was organised by Josef Goebbels. The Nazis used the latest technology – loudspeakers, slide shows and films – to spread their message. In the 1932 election campaign they even used planes to make sure that Hitler could speak in as many places as possible.

The mass rallies that the Nazis held also helped to win them support. Music, lighting and marches gave the impression of discipline and order in a time of chaos. The Nazis also used powerful propaganda posters with simple slogans, like the one shown here, to spread their key ideas.

Source 4

'Our last hope: Hitler'. A Nazi election poster from 1932

OTHER EVENTS

The opposing team have put forward some important points, but there is more to our case than just the Wall Street Crash. We feel that three other **important factors** helped the Nazis get into power.

A

FEAR OF COMMUNISM

Fear of Communism.
I believe that the Nazis were very lucky to receive so much support. Many people voted for them because they were scared of the Communists getting into power. The Nazis seemed to be the only party who could stop the Communists.

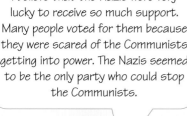

From 1930 to 1932 support for the Communists increased. The German Communist Party was the largest in Europe, outside the Soviet Union. Many people in Germany feared they would take over the country. The Communists had a lot of support from the working class and close links with the Soviet Union. But German business owners and farmers feared the Communists because in the Soviet Union the Communist government had taken over big industries and farmers' land.

B

WEAK OPPOSITION

Weak opposition.
The Nazis were also fortunate that their opponents were so weak. Stronger opposition would have made it a lot more difficult for the Nazis to get into power.

Opposition to the Nazis was weak and divided. The Nazis' two main rivals, the Communist Party and the Social Democratic Party, were bitter enemies. They were not prepared to work together to stop the Nazis. People had lost trust in the parties who had ruled Germany during the Great Depression. They did not seem to be able to do anything to solve the crisis. To make matters worse, they argued amongst themselves about what to do. They did not offer strong, effective leadership.

Finally, we must remember that Hitler became Chancellor because of a **political deal** with the leader of another party. Without this deal he woud not have been able to become Chancellor. Whether or not Hitler became Chancellor remained in the balance until the very last moment.

C A POLITICAL DEAL

1 NAZI SUCCESS

In July 1932 the Nazis won 37 per cent of the vote in the elections. They were the largest party in the Reichstag. However, the Nazis did not have the majority they needed to control the Reichstag.

2 ENTER PAPEN

Hitler demanded to be made Chancellor. However, Paul von Hindenburg (the President) refused. Instead, he appointed his friend, Franz von Papen (leader of the Catholic Centre Party), as Chancellor. Papen soon faced many problems. He did not have the support of the Reichstag.

3 ENTER SCHLEICHER

General von Schleicher persuaded Hindenburg to remove Papen. In December, Schleicher became Chancellor.

4 PAPEN'S REVENGE!

Papen wanted revenge. He was determined to get back into power and remove Schleicher. The Nazis were still the largest party so Papen thought he could use them to get power for himself. He met with Hitler and made a political deal. They agreed to form a new government, with Hitler as Chancellor and Papen as Vice-Chancellor. Wealthy businessmen went along with the plan because they believed that Papen, not Hitler, would control the new government.

5 ENTER HITLER

Papen persuaded Hindenburg to agree to his plan. In January 1933 Hitler became Chancellor. Hindenburg and Papen thought that they could control Hitler. They made sure that only three out of the twelve people who made up the new government were Nazis.

Why did some Germans change their minds and vote for Hitler?

Why might people who would *not* have supported the Nazis in 1928 have changed their minds by 1932?

Discuss

Here are the five people whom you first met on page 33. Study what has happened to each of them between 1928 and 1932.

a) Which people who would not have supported the Nazis in 1928 might support them now? Why do you think their views might have changed?

b) Which people who would not have supported the Nazis in 1928 would still not do so now? Why do you think their views would not have changed?

Dietrich

I have lost my job working in the factory. Like most of my friends I am now unemployed. My landlord has kicked me out of my flat because I could not afford the rent. The government is doing nothing to help. They don't care about people like me. The Nazis are the only party who seem to be doing anything. The SA have been running soup kitchens and they have put some of my friends up in a hostel.

Josef

My business is really struggling. People just don't have the money to spend any more. Demand for goods has dropped and so have my profits. I have had to lay off a lot of workers. The situation at the moment really scares me. Hitler blames the crisis on the Jews. With so much bitterness and anger about, people are starting to listen to him. They want someone to blame. I am worried about the safety of my family.

Maria

I have not been able to get a job since I left university. I am well-qualified, but with so much unemployment there is little hope for people like me. My boyfriend and I are living in a tent in the local park whilst the rich still live life to the full. The only good news is that support for the Communists is growing. The Nazis keep trying to break up our meetings but many workers are starting to listen to our message.

Franz

Helga

My husband's factory has gone bankrupt. The loans that he depended on stopped after the Wall Street Crash. Many of the banks have gone bankrupt too. There is no hope of my husband raising enough money to set up another business. We're having to live off our savings. The government is useless. The different parties spend too long arguing amongst themselves. What we need is a strong leader who can sort out the mess that we are in. Gangs of workers hang around on the streets and there is a lot of violence. I really fear that the Communists could take over. People are desperate and are starting to look for drastic alternatives.

The farmer that I used to work for has gone bankrupt. Food prices had been falling for a number of years. The depression made the situation even worse. It was impossible for small farms such as his to survive. I am grateful that he kept me on as long as he did. I have moved in with my parents because I cannot afford a house of my own. It is hard for my parents. They help me out as much as they can, but the government has cut their pension payments again.

'The Wall Street Crash was the main reason Hitler got into power.'
Do you agree? [16]

You may use the following in your answer:

- In 1928 the Nazis received less than 3 per cent of the vote.
- In 1932 unemployment in Germany reached 16 per cent.
- A Nazi election poster had the slogan: 'Hitler – our last hope'.

You will meet high-scoring questions like this as Question 5b or 6b on your paper. We began looking at them on page 27. Now let's go a bit further into how to get lots of those 16 marks.

You need to be careful not to be led astray by this type of question. We call it an 'ICEBERG QUESTION' because, like an iceberg, there is more to it than meets the eye! Many students think that a question such as this only requires them to write about the Wall Street Crash. This would be very dangerous. Do not spend your whole answer dealing with the impact of the Wall Street Crash. Look at the question carefully. You have to explore if the Wall Street Crash was 'the main reason' why Hitler got into power. In order to do this properly you must look at other factors as well.

We will return to answering this kind of question on page 62.

We will return to answering this kind of question on page 62.

Activity

Follow the steps below to safely negotiate this iceberg question!

What about the bullet points?

The three bullet points are meant to be helpful hints, but students are often unsure how to use them.

Here are some tips:

- They are NOT the plan for your answer.
- You don't even HAVE TO use them at all…
- …But they are hints of items you might like to include.
- In this case, the item about Nazis only receiving 3 per cent of the vote in 1928 could go in your opening sentence.
- The unemployment figure in the second bullet point follows on from the bit of the iceberg you can see (see Step 1 in the diagram below).
- The Nazi slogan in the third bullet point shows how Hitler made use of the hardship of the Great Depression in his propaganda.
- The REAL plan for a good answer can be found Steps 1, 2 and 3 in the diagram below.

Step 1: Deal with the part of the question that is above the surface.
- Explain how the Wall Street Crash helped Hitler get into power.
- Link the Great Depression to growing support for extreme parties such as the Nazis.

Step 2: Deal with the part of the question that lurks beneath the surface. You could include:
- The role played by Hitler
- Nazi Party organisation, promises and propaganda
- Fear of Communism and weak opposition
- The political deal between Papen and Hitler.

Step 3: Write your conclusion. DO NOT SIT ON THE FENCE!
What was the *key factor* in Hitler's rise to power? Was it the Wall Street Crash or something more important?

2.1 How was Hitler able to become dictator?

In January 1933 Hitler became Chancellor of Germany. By August 1934 democracy in Germany was dead and Hitler was dictator. How did he do this? You will discover the sequence of events that brought this about and make a 'living graph' of Nazi power to show how Hitler was able to destroy democracy.

How strong was Hitler's position in January 1933?

When Hitler became Chancellor he was in a very weak position.

- Support for the Nazis had fallen from 37 per cent to 33 per cent during 1932. In order to control the Reichstag, Hitler needed over 50 per cent of the vote. He was a long way from achieving this.
- Hitler could be sacked by President Hindenburg at any time.
- Apart from Hitler, only two other Nazis had been given positions in the new government. The nine other positions were filled by non-Nazis whom Hindenburg and Papen thought they could control.
- Hindenburg and Papen planned to use Hitler like a puppet. Papen boasted to a friend, 'In two months we will have pushed Hitler into a corner so that he squeaks'.

Discuss

What does Source 1 suggest about the position Hitler found himself in when he became Chancellor?

Source 1

◀ This cartoon appeared in a Social Democratic Party newspaper on 1 February 1933. The cartoon is called 'Hugenberg's Driving School'. Hugenberg, a member of the German National Party, is saying to Papen: 'That newcomer up there in front can imagine all he wants that he's steering but we'll set the economic course!'

18 months later...

By the end of 1934 Hitler was in a totally different position.

- Papen had resigned.
- Hindenburg was dead and Hitler was now President, as well as Chancellor.
- The army had taken an oath of personal loyalty to Hitler.
- The Nazis were the only political party.
- All threats to the Nazi Party had been removed.
- Hitler had the power to introduce any law he wanted.

How did this happen?

smarter revision: Living graphs

Using information from pages 48–49, you are going to construct a 'living graph' like this, which charts how Hitler increased his power between January 1933 and August 1934.

- You will need to use A3 paper.
- Think carefully about where you plot each event.
- Use bullet points to explain your thinking and support the decisions you make.

When you have finished, answer the following questions.

1 Which of the following periods do you think was the most important:
   - February 1933–March 1933
   - May 1933–July 1933
   - June 1934–August 1934?

   Write a sentence to explain your answer.

2 Mark on your living graph three turning points that led to a significant increase in Hitler's power. Rank them in order of importance and write a paragraph to explain your decision.

3 You could use a living graph to help you remember other events in this course too. For example, use Section 1.3 to show how little the Nazis had achieved between 1919 and 1928 (pages 28–34).

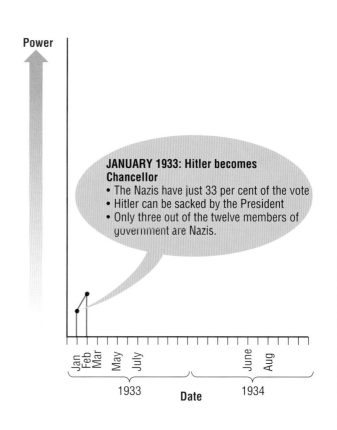

JANUARY 1933: Hitler becomes Chancellor
- The Nazis have just 33 per cent of the vote
- Hitler can be sacked by the President
- Only three out of the twelve members of government are Nazis.

Hitler's path to dictatorship

27 February – Reichstag fire

The Reichstag building in Berlin was destroyed by fire. Marinus van der Lubbe, a Dutch Communist, was found at the scene. He appeared to have been acting alone but the Nazis claimed that this was the start of a Communist plot to take over Germany. That night 4000 Communist leaders were arrested by the police. The next day Hitler persuaded Hindenburg to grant him emergency powers. This gave the police the power to arrest people and hold them for as long as they wanted, without trial. Thousands of people who opposed the Nazi Party were arrested. The Nazis also banned meetings held by their political opponents and closed down their newspapers.

5 March – New elections

The Nazis used the police and the SA to put pressure on their political opponents. More than 50 opponents of the Nazis were killed and many more were injured. The Nazis used radio to broadcast their anti-Communist message. This helped the Nazis achieve their best ever election result, with 44 per cent of the vote.

24 March – The Enabling Act

Hitler wanted still more. He wanted an Enabling Act. This law would give Hitler the power to pass laws without going through the Reichstag or the President. This law would place all the power in his hands.

In order to achieve this he needed to get two-thirds of the Reichstag to support it. They had to be persuaded to give up their power and hand it to Hitler! How did he achieve this?

The Communist Party were banned from voting. The Centre Party were persuaded to vote in favour of the law as Hitler promised to protect the Catholic Church. Only the Social Democrats voted against it. The Enabling Act was passed by 444 votes to 94.

The Weimar Republic and the democracy it brought to Germany had ended. The Reichstag had voted itself out of existence. Germany was now a dictatorship. All important decisions would be made by Hitler and his closest advisers.

2 May – Trade unions taken over

Trade union offices were taken over and union leaders arrested. All trade unions were merged into one organisation, the new German Labour Front (DAF). The DAF was controlled by the Nazis.

July – All political parties banned

A law was introduced that banned people from forming new political parties. By this stage the Social Democratic Party and the Communist Party had already been banned. Other political parties had broken up. This new law meant that no new parties could be set up to challenge the Nazis. There was now only one party in Germany.

COMMUNIST PARTY MANIFESTO BANNED

GERMAN DEMOCRATIC PARTY MANIFESTO BANNED

SOCIAL DEMOCRATIC PARTY MANIFESTO BANNED

1934

29–30 June – Night of the Long Knives

By 1934 Hitler had become concerned at the increasing power of the SA. It had over 3 million members and wanted to take control of the army. The leader of the SA, Ernst Röhm, was a close friend of Hitler's. However, Hitler thought that Röhm was a potential rival.

Hitler had another reason for attacking the SA. He needed to reassure the army. The army was smaller than the SA but it was well-trained and disciplined. It was the only organisation that had the power to overthrow Hitler. Army leaders feared being taken over by the SA and resented the violence they used. The army was supported by powerful businessmen who wanted Hitler to expand the army and buy new weapons.

On the Night of the Long Knives, SA leaders were dragged from their beds, taken to Nazi headquarters and shot dead. Röhm too was arrested. When he refused to commit suicide, he was shot in prison. The Night of the Long Knives sent a warning to the rest of Germany about how ruthless Hitler was in his pursuit of power.

2 August – Death of Hindenburg

When Hindenburg died, Hitler made himself President as well as Chancellor. He was now the undisputed head of the government and took the title *Führer* (Supreme Leader).

August – Army oath

The army took an oath of personal loyalty to Hitler. Hitler was now Supreme Commander of the armed forces. All German soldiers swore to obey Hitler and to risk their life for him at any time.

How was Hitler able to increase his power between January 1933 and August 1934? [12]

You may use the following in your answer and any other information of your own:

- February 1933 The Reichstag Fire
- July 1933 All political parties banned
- August 1934 Death of Hindenburg

You will meet questions like this as Question 3 or 4 on your paper (you will have a choice). You can see that it is worth 12 marks, so you need to give it some time – nearly 20 minutes. We have already looked at one example of this style of question on page 35, where we concentrated on **relevance**. You might like to look back at the advice and examples on that page.

First of all, a warning: the danger is that you just tell the story of what was going on in Germany between the two dates. But the question is about **how Hitler increased his power**.

WARNING

DO NOT TELL A STORY

Avoid danger … use connectives!

A good answer to this question will link events with their results. You can do this by using **result connectives** in each paragraph. You can see some examples of this underlined in 'Improve that answer'. Result connectives can help you tie your answer together. They make sure that you **explain why** something took place rather than just telling a story.

In January 1933 Hitler was in a weak position. President Hindenburg could sack him at any time and he had only 33 per cent of the vote. In February 1933 the Reichstag was burnt down by a Dutch Communist called Marinus van der Lubbe. The Nazis claimed that this was part of a Communist plot to take over Germany.

This meant that Hitler was able to persuade Hindenburg to grant him Emergency Powers. Hitler used these powers to attack Communists and political opponents. This led to the Nazis achieving their best ever election result in March 1933.

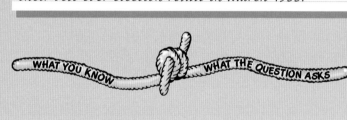

WHAT YOU KNOW   WHAT THE QUESTION ASKS

Useful result connectives

This meant that…

This led to…

It enabled him to…

He could now…

This resulted in…

In March 1933 there was a new election and the Nazis achieved their best ever result. The Nazis gained 44 per cent of the vote but Hitler still did not have the majority he wanted in the Reichstag. However, later in the month he persuaded the Reichstag to pass the Enabling Law.

In May Hitler took over the trade unions and in July he banned all other political parties.

This meant that...
(Explain why the Enabling Law was so important.)

The Enabling Law resulted in Hitler being able to...

How should you use the three bullet points?

All questions like this provide three bullet points of items 'you may use'. They are intended to be helpful, to get you thinking about what to include in your answer. But how do you use them?

- You don't have to use all three, but you will probably find you can include them all in your answer without stretching it. In most cases – as here – it would be hard to think of a good answer that didn't include all three items.

- Remember to connect. Writing all you can remember about the three items does not help to explain how Hitler was able to increase his power. You need to connect each one to what the question is about. (Use the connectives at the bottom of page 50 to help you.)

- The three bullets are **not** the plan for your answer. You should make a plan of your own and include the three items where you think they fit best.

- You will certainly have to add in some information of your own, as the question suggests. Look back to pages 48 and 49. These are eight events there, but only three bullet points in the question. A really good answer would bring all of the other five items.

Activity

- Write your own answer to the question.
- You could start with the student's answer in the 'Improve that answer' boxes, adding in the two improvement sections on this page.
- You could bring in the third bullet point, and any of the other events from pages 48 and 49 which you think are important.
- Or, you could start your own answer from scratch. You could vary the pattern of each paragraph by starting with the way an item increased Hitler's power and then going on to provide supporting details.

2.2 How did Hitler keep control?

From 1933 to 1945 the Nazis faced almost no challenges to their rule from the German people. You must decide whether this was because people were frightened into obedience or were simply persuaded by Nazi propaganda.

Hitler did not rule Germany on his own. In fact, he didn't work very hard. His normal routine was to get up late, go for a stroll in the morning, chat to friends over a long lunch, do a bit of work, have dinner and watch a film before going to bed late. Those 'chats' often included making important decisions, but other people carried them out. They were 'Hitler's henchmen': the powerful people who actually controlled the Nazi empire.

Two of Hitler's henchmen stand out: Himmler and Goebbels. But who was more important?

Activity

You are an editor for a book publisher. Your boss, Ms Hodray, wants to publish a bestseller called *Hitler's Henchmen*. But whose picture should go on the cover – Himmler or Goebbels?

Over the next five pages it is your job to find out who was more important. Rank each aspect of control out of five, to show how important you think it was.

Complete your own copy of the tables below and then prepare an oral presentation to convince Ms Hodray that your choice should go on the cover. Ms Hodray is tough, so you have to be clear about the reasons for your choice – and why you rejected the other one.

Himmler – control by terror	How this helped control Germany	Supporting evidence	Rating out of 5
SS			
Concentration camps			
Gestapo			
The police			
Local wardens			

Goebbels – control by propaganda	How this helped control Germany	Supporting evidence	Rating out of 5
Newspapers			
Rallies			
Books			
Radio			
Films			

Childhood	• Born in 1900, the son of a teacher
	• Did well at school
Appearance and character	• Timid, frail and clumsy. People said he looked like a quiet, small-town bank clerk
	• Hard worker and efficient organiser
	• Clever at building up his own power
	• Although he took overall control of the Holocaust, he fainted at the sight of Jews being killed
Early career	• Joined German army in 1918: did not fight
	• Failed to make a living as a poultry farmer
	• Joined the Nazi Party in 1923. Took part in the Munich Putsch in the same year
Role in Nazi Germany	• 1929: made head of the SS – Hitler's private army
	• 1936: made head of all police in Nazi Germany, including the Gestapo (the secret police)
	• 1941: set up the Death's Head units of the SS that ran slave labour camps and carried out the mass murder of Jews

HEINRICH HIMMLER

OR...

Childhood	• Born in 1897, the son of a poor manual worker
	• Crippled by polio as a child
Appearance and character	• Small, walked with a limp as a result of polio
	• Intelligent and well-educated
	• Good speaker – second only to Hitler
	• Spoke in favour of family life and simplicity, but often visited nightclubs, had mistresses and owned several houses
Early career	• Declared medically unfit to fight in the First World War
	• He tried to make a living as a playwright, then turned to journalism
	• Joined the Nazi Party in 1922. At first he opposed Hitler, but later supported him
Role in Nazi Germany	• 1928: put in charge of Nazi propaganda. Brilliant propaganda designer and thinker
	• 1938: gave orders for Kristallnacht (attack on Jewish property; see page 83)
	• 1943: put in complete charge of the war effort. As defeat loomed he helped to organise 'total war', raising morale and help for victims of the Allied bombings

JOSEF GOEBBELS

Discuss

Before you start...
From just these outlines, who seems the more likely candidate for the book cover? Why?

Control by terror?

The Nazis tried to make the German people feel too afraid to express any kind of criticism or opposition. At the centre of this network of terror was Himmler.

The SS

SS stands for 'Schutz Staffel', which means protection squad. The black-uniformed SS was originally Hitler's personal bodyguard. Himmler built it up and by 1939 it had 240,000 members. All recruits had to be recognisably 'Aryan' – blond, blue-eyed and physically fit. Himmler imposed high physical standards: even having a filled tooth was enough to disqualify you. Himmler trained the SS to be ruthless and fiercely loyal to Hitler. They could arrest people without trial and could search houses.

Concentration camps

As soon as the Nazi Party came to power the SS arrested many Nazi opponents and put them in temporary prisons. Then special concentration camps were constructed, usually in remote rural areas.

At first, inmates were held in the camps for short periods of questioning, torture, hard labour and forced instruction in Nazi ideas. By the late 1930s concentration camps were being run by a section of the SS called Death's Head units, as forced labour camps. Some prisoners were used to work for Nazi-owned businesses. Himmler controlled over 150 companies who used slave labour to make all kinds of goods, including weapons.

The camps held Jews, Communists, Socialists, trade unionists, church leaders – anyone who criticised the Nazis.

Source 1

▲ Nazi opponents being questioned in a concentration camp, 1933

The Gestapo

This was the state secret police. They could tap telephones, open mail and collect information from a huge network of informers. Informers reported on local people who they believed were 'anti-Nazi'. The Gestapo arrested people without trial, tortured them and imprisoned them in concentration camps.

The police

The ordinary police continued with their regular work, but their bosses were all Nazis. This meant that the police became part of the network of informers, collecting information on everyone, whilst ignoring crimes committed by Nazis.

Source 2

▲ A teletype room in Gestapo headquarters, where information was received from informers

Source 3

▲ SS guards after taking over the Berlin broadcasting station in 1933.

Local wardens

The Nazi Party had a strong local structure. Every town was divided into small units, called blocks. The Block Warden, a local Nazi, visited every home in the block each week, collecting donations to the Nazi Party and checking up on everyone.

As a Socialist opponent of Hitler said, 'Every staircase has an informer.' The Block Warden wrote a report on everyone in their block. This report could affect whether or not you got a job. The Warden noted any signs of independent thinking, for example, not flying the Nazi flag on celebration days, or not being enthusiastic enough about Hitler and his achievements.

Control by propaganda?

In 1924 Hitler laid out his beliefs and his plans for successful propaganda in his book, *Mein Kampf* (see Source 4). In 1928 he chose Josef Goebbels to run the Nazi Ministry of Propaganda.

Goebbels put Hitler's approach to propaganda into practice brilliantly. He took control of all the mass media. He made sure newspapers and posters carried the strong, simple, repeated slogans of the Nazis. Through censorship he prevented the German people from hearing any conflicting messages.

Source 4

From *Mein Kampf*, by Adolf Hitler
The powers of understanding of the masses are feeble. And they quickly forget. So effective propaganda has to be limited to a few bare essentials and these must be as simple as possible. These slogans should be repeated until the very last person has come to grasp the idea.

Newspapers

Anti-Nazi newspapers were shut down. Jews were banned from owning or working for newspapers. Goebbels' Ministry of Propaganda sent out daily instructions to all remaining newspapers telling them what to print, what kind of pictures should be published and what angle they should take on the news. Display boards were set up in public places so that everyone could read these newspapers.

Activity

Use the information on these two pages to fill out your table for Goebbels.

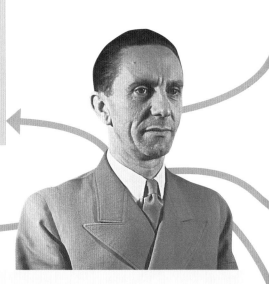

Rallies

Source 5

The Nazis always presented an image of order and control to the German people, with their uniforms, meetings, torchlight processions and rallies. Once they were in power, they made their rallies even more impressive. A huge stadium at Nuremberg was specially built for them. Goebbels stage-managed these rallies to give a dramatic impression of overwhelming power and unity.

◀ Nuremberg rally, 1937. There are 100,000 Nazis here, with 32,000 flags. Around the edge of the stadium, 150 searchlights create a spectacular effect

Radio

Goebbels took over control of all radio broadcasting. Regular programmes included Hitler's speeches, German music and German history – foreign programmes could not be picked up. Cheap radios were made so that as many Germans as possible could listen to Nazi propaganda. By 1939 70 per cent of Germans owned a radio. Loudspeakers were set up in public squares all over Germany and people were encouraged to listen to important radio programmes and announcements.

Source 6

Newspaper advertisement, 1934
Attention! The Führer is speaking on the radio! On Wednesday 21 March, the Führer is speaking on all German stations from 11.00 a.m. to 11.50 a.m. Nazi Party headquarters have ordered that all factory-owners, department stores, offices, shops, pubs and blocks of flats put up loudspeakers an hour before the broadcast so that the whole workforce can participate fully in the broadcast.

Books

As soon as they came to power, the Nazis organised official book-burnings – books were burned in public on massive bonfires. The Nazis burned:

- books by Communists and Socialists
- books by Jews
- books by anyone they disapproved of
- books containing ideas they disapproved of.

By burning books the Nazis were preventing German people from reading and thinking beyond the Nazi message. All new books published had to be censored by Goebbels' Ministry.

Source 7

Book-burning, 1933 ▶

Source 8

▲ A Dutch poster for *The Eternal Jew* (in German *Der ewige Jude*), 1940

Films

The cinema was very popular in most countries in the 1930s. Goebbels controlled all of the films made in Germany. Most were adventure stories, comedies or love stories, but there was always a newsreel film, *News of the Week*. The newsreels were made by Goebbels' film-makers and shown before the main film.

Some openly pro-Nazi films were made on Goebbels' orders and with strict control of the scripts. Source 8 is a poster for *The Eternal Jew*, an anti-Semitic film made by the Nazis.

Activity

So, who do you think was more important in keeping the German people under control: Himmler – the master of terror; or Goebbels – the master of propaganda? You may already have decided. But here's the catch. In your presentation to the scary Ms Hodray half of you must argue for Himmler, half of you for Goebbels – whatever you really think.

Step one: prepare your case
You have done most of the work for this by filling in the two tables from page 52. Look over them again – not just the one about your choice, but the table for the rejected henchman too.
- For your chosen man, which aspect did you rate as most important? Are you going to start with that?
- Or save it to the end, as a real clincher? Read your supporting evidence. Which will make the most powerful impression?
- Check out the opposition. Look at the table for your rejected henchman. What are his strong points? Ms Hodray will almost certainly fire these at you to try to prove that you have made the wrong choice. How will you counter her arguments?
- Finally, make a clear plan of your running order.

Step two: write your speech
- This double burger reminds you of the structure of a good speech.
- Be selective. You have a limited amount of time: don't try to say everything.

Step three: practise your presentation
- Run through your presentation, out loud, to a partner or on your own. Listen to criticism and be prepared to make changes.
- Make sure you can pronounce key words.
- Emphasise key points, for example, by repetition, or by choosing powerful words.
- Use persuasive words and phrases, such as: 'The evidence clearly demonstrates. . .' rather than 'The evidence shows. . .'.

Step four: prepare for any opposition
- Be prepared to defend your point of view. Be sure you really understand the points you want to make.
- Try to guess what opposing views might be, and how to crush them.

Step five: during the presentation
- Listen to any opposing views. Jot down questions and points you disagree with.
- Try to find evidence to dispute points made in favour of the other candidate.

Step six: afterwards
- Review how it went. What did you do well? What could you improve upon?

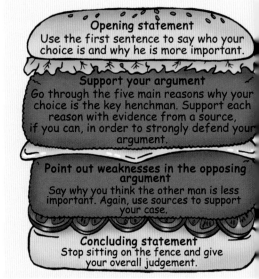

Opening statement
Use the first sentence to say who your choice is and why he is more important.

Support your argument
Go through the five main reasons why your choice is the key henchman. Support each reason with evidence from a source, if you can, in order to strongly defend your argument.

Point out weaknesses in the opposing argument
Say why you think the other man is less important. Again, use sources to support your case.

Concluding statement
Stop sitting on the fence and give your overall judgement.

Those who fell in line with the Nazis

Source 1

▲ German judges give the Nazi salute as they swear loyalty to Hitler

Discuss

Many Germans simply fell in line with the Nazis. Here are some important groups who did so. Why do you think they fell in line? Was it terror, propaganda – or something else?

Lawyers, judges and courts

All Jewish judges and lawyers were removed. Judges had to be Nazi Party members, so a fair trial was impossible. The number of offences carrying the death penalty went up from three in 1933 to 46 by 1943. Nazi laws had to be enforced, for example, listening to foreign radio stations, telling an anti-Nazi joke, and having a sexual relationship with a Jew all became illegal activities.

The Churches

Roman Catholics – in 1933 Hitler made an agreement with the Roman Catholic Church that it would not interfere in politics. In return the Nazis would leave them alone.

Protestants – the Nazis hoped to bring the Protestant Church under Nazi control. A 'Reich Church' was set up, with the slogan 'With the swastika on our chests and the cross in our hearts'. Reich Church pastors had to swear an oath of loyalty to Hitler. Many Protestant ministers objected, and in 1934 set up their own 'Confessional Church' outside Nazi control.

We have seen that Hitler was determined to control the lives and minds of young people. Therefore, in spite of his promises to leave the Churches alone, in 1936 all Church youth groups were stopped and by 1939 nearly all Church schools had been closed down.

Overall, Church opposition to the Nazis was very cautious: they did not, for example, criticise Kristallnacht (see page 83). Only 50 pastors (out of 17,000) and one bishop were actually put in prison for opposition activities or speeches.

Source 2

▲ Bishop Ludwig Mueller, head of the Reich Church, gives the Nazi salute, surrounded by uniformed Nazis.

Meet the Examiner: Making inferences from a source

Give **two** things that you can learn from Source A about Nazi propaganda. [4]

We looked at a question like this, which comes as Question 1 on your paper, on page 26 and explained that the key skill here is **inference**. That is, using all the clues in the source to find evidence which isn't immediately obvious from the words or the picture. There are two steps to this.

Step 1: What does the source tell you? Look for clues in the source to help you.

Step 2: What do the clues in this source **suggest** about Nazi propaganda? Go beyond the obvious clues and ask yourself: What can I **infer** from this source about the kind of image of Hitler the painting is trying to give?

Obvious clues:

Other soldiers are being called on to join the group.

Hitler is surrounded by soldiers and airmen.

Most of the men are shown as blond, blue-eyed, handsome.

Source A

▲ A painting of Hitler with German soldiers and airmen

Inferences:

Nazi propaganda was designed to show that:
Hitler is popular.

Hitler mixes easily with fighting men.

The German armed forces are made up of Aryans.

Answering an inference question in the exam

- **Find two inferences.** There are only 4 marks for this question, so don't spend too long on it: two is all the question asks for.

- **Refer to details in the source to support the inference you have made.** If you don't support your inferences from the source you only get 2 marks, so be sure to collect all 4.

Activity

Now write **two more** supported inferences from this source.

The source suggests that Nazi propaganda aimed to show that Hitler is popular. For example, they are gathered around him, mainly looking at him, and others are being beckoned to join them.

> The boxes below show two important aspects of Nazi rule.
>
> Choose **one** and explain its importance in giving the Nazis control of Germany. [9]
>
> | **From 1933 rallies were held at Nuremberg** | **Himmler headed the SS 1934–1945** |

You will meet questions like this as Question 2 on your exam paper. You can see that you have a bit of choice: choose one of the boxed items only. With 9 marks, this is quite an important question: give it 13–14 minutes.

Proving importance – the keys to success

Stick to the content focus of the question

Whichever item you choose, you have to show how it contributed to **Nazi control of Germany**. If you chose 'Rallies' there is plenty you could write about them: the pageantry, the flags, the uniforms, the discipline, the special stadium at Nuremberg and so on. And the most you could get for those details would be 3 marks out of 9 – because they do not address the **content focus of the question**. You have to write about Rallies and **the part they played in giving the Nazis control of Germany**.

Prove it was important

On pages 54–57 several items are described which helped the Nazis control Germany. But which were really **important**? You need to show that the item you have chosen was really important.

Activity

1 Work in groups. Take one boxed item each and use the Keys to Success to answer the question.
2 Produce a draft answer from each group. Check each other's draft.
 • Does the answer focus on the question?
 • Does it explain how important the chosen item was?
3 Provide feedback for each other and improve each other's draft answer.

Meet the examiner: The 16-mark question 3 – analysing causes

Here is another opportunity to get to grips with the last question on the paper, the one worth the biggest number of marks: Question 5(b) or 6(b). You have a choice about which one you do, but it is worth 16 marks. Doing well on this question alone will probably affect your grade. Give it about 25 minutes, and include in that some thinking and planning time.

On page 27 we looked at the importance of writing a **balanced** answer and on page 45 we looked at **icebergs**. Here we are going to look at how you actually put an excellent answer together.

'The use of propaganda was the main reason why the Nazis were able to control the German people.'

Do you agree? Explain your answer. [16]

You may use the following in your answer and any other information of your own:

- 1928 Goebbels put in charge of Nazi propaganda

- 1933 first concentration camp set up

- 1939 70 per cent of all Germans own a radio

As we have seen, in this style of question you are given one cause – the sentence in inverted commas. It is a piece of bait, dangled in front of your nose. Are you going to swallow it whole? It sounds right, doesn't it?

In fact such a statement is always partly right – and partly wrong. It's another 'iceberg question' (see page 45). Here only propaganda is mentioned – the 'visible' part of the iceberg – but to score well you have to write about the 'unseen' part too – terror.

So your answer will have two main parts:

1 Information which supports the statement – this will be about propaganda

2 Information which gives the other side – this will be about the fear factor.

And you will need an introduction and a conclusion as well.

In your introduction it is often a good idea to pick up the wording of the question in your opening sentence. It keeps you from wandering off the point and shows the examiner that you intend to answer the question. For example:

> *Propaganda was certainly an important factor in helping the Nazis to control the German people. They used propaganda to persuade the German people that Nazi rule was the best thing for Germany.*

Part one

In this part you find good examples of how Nazi propaganda was used to control the German people. You could write a paragraph each about two or three of the main methods the Nazis used – newspapers, films, books, rallies and radio. Note that you are given 'radio' in one of the bullets, but you have to explain how it was used, AND you have to add some examples of your own. The student's answer on the right does this well. The first sentence makes clear what the paragraph is going to be about, then adds some well-selected detail and ends by linking this information to the main theme – control.

One important method of propaganda was the radio. This was also under Goebbels' control and cheap radios were manufactured so that most Germans could receive Nazi propaganda. People were encouraged to listen to important programmes like Hitler's speeches. Loudspeakers in public squares also made it almost impossible to escape the Nazi message.

Select from your own knowledge to support your answer

Part two

This will need to start with a strong 'turning-the-corner' connective to show that you are not going to swallow the bait, that you know that there is more to the question than has been mentioned so far. Here is an example using the connective 'however'.

On pages 54–55 you looked at five different means of terror used by the Nazis to control the German people. Note down four key facts from those pages which you could include. Then use these and your own knowledge to write the rest of part two.

However, propaganda was not the only factor enabling the Nazis to control the German people. The Nazis also made the German people afraid that if they stepped out of line terrible things would happen to them.

'Turning-the-corner' connective

Conclusion

Now think what your final opinion is on this question: was propaganda the main factor? Or was terror?

And how firm do you want to be? Note that the question says 'how far do you agree...?'

If you are very firm, you could use emphasising connectives such as:

It is clear that...
What is certain...

Don't write too much in your conclusion: three sentences is enough. But it is a good opportunity to show that you have something to say and can put forward a clear argument.

If you want to show that the answer is still debatable, you could use conceding connectives such as:

It seems that...
Perhaps...
It is possible that...

2.3 Why was opposition to the Nazis so weak?

You may have the impression that there was no opposition at all to the Nazis, but that was not the case. In this section you will find out about five different opposition groups. You will think about how each one opposed Hitler and which one posed the biggest threat to Nazi power. At the end you will draw a diagram to summarise the reasons why opposition to the Nazis was weak and ineffective.

The Nazis did not want any opposition. In their ideal Germany all Germans would work together to achieve the same goals – the Nazi goals. Within days of taking power Hitler banned all other political parties. The normal democratic right to oppose or protest against a government was not going to be allowed.

The Gestapo

As we saw on page 55, the Gestapo made it their business to find out about Nazi opponents. They tapped phones, opened letters and spied on suspects. A network of Nazi informers passed on information to them. Suspected opponents were arrested and, if part of a wider network, were tortured until they revealed the names of everyone in their group.

Activity

On the next five pages you will find Gestapo 'information files', like this, about each opposition group. As you read them, think about how much of a threat each one posed to Hitler and the Nazis. On your own copy of this table give each group a 'danger rating' (!!!!! very dangerous; ! no threat at all).

GESTAPO SECRET FILE

Group	Methods used to oppose the Nazis	Danger rating	Reasons why you have given that score
Former political opponents			
The Churches			
Army officers			
Edelweiss Pirates			
White Rose Group			

GESTAPO SECRET FILE

OPPOSITION GROUPS
1 Former political opponents

SUPPORT: The Socialist Party, the Communist Party and the trade unions. They were, of course, our main enemies in the Weimar Republic. They were huge organisations in those days. The parties lost the elections of 1933 but still have millions of members. So do the trade unions.

AIMS: Restoration of democracy, free speech and workers' democratic rights. The Communists want a workers' revolution.

ACTIVITIES: Secret meetings, strikes, handing out leaflets, writing anti-Nazi graffiti on walls.

WHEN MOST ACTIVE: 1933–1935

What happened...

All opposition parties and trade unions were banned by July 1933. Their offices were raided, ransacked and closed. Thousands of Socialists, including members of the Reichstag and former ministers as well as trade union officials, were arrested and put in concentration camps. Many were beaten up; some were tortured; a few were killed. Most were soon released. The aim was to scare people into joining the Nazis, or at least into keeping quiet.

In the years immediately after 1933, working-class opposition to Nazism continued: from 1933 to 1935 there were 400 strikes. However, the Gestapo continued to make mass arrests – for example, two-thirds of all Communist Party members were arrested. Many died in the camps. Many more went into exile abroad. Socialist, Communist and trade union organisations were forced underground, holding secret meetings, occasionally handing out leaflets, waiting for the day when democracy would return to Germany.

Source 1

◀ Political prisoners in a concentration camp near Berlin

GESTAPO SECRET FILE

OPPOSITION GROUPS
2 The Churches

SUPPORT: About 22 million people belong to the Roman Catholic Church – 32 per cent of the population. About 40 million belong to Protestant Churches – 58 per cent of the population. There are other, smaller Christian Churches, too.

The Churches are by far the largest non-Nazi organisation left in Germany after 1933. They have bishops to lead them and a priest or pastor in every parish, to whom many ordinary Germans look for guidance.

AIMS: These are large organisations embracing a variety of political views. Some church leaders actively support the Nazis, some actively oppose them. Most are somewhere in-between and want to keep religion and politics separate. Some just want to keep their important positions.

ACTIVITIES: They carry out baptisms, marriages and burials. The Churches also run many schools: two-thirds of all German children go to a Church school.

WHEN MOST ACTIVE: Throughout the whole Nazi period, 1933–1945

What happened...

Bishop von Galen was the Roman Catholic Bishop of Munster. He openly criticised Nazi racial policy in his sermons as early as 1934. In 1941 his outrage against Nazi euthanasia policy led to its being halted. He was so popular that the Nazis dared not remove him. However, some priests were executed for handing out copies of his sermons.

Dietrich Bonhöffer pointed out that Nazism was anti-Christian as early as 1933. His job was training young men to be ministers. He taught them that you cannot, and should not, separate religion and politics and that true religion is standing up to a corrupt or evil government. The Nazis closed his college in 1940. He could have escaped to Britain, where he had many friends, but chose to stay and speak out against Nazism. He was arrested in 1943 and executed in 1945. His ideas have been influential throughout the world since his death.

Martin Niemöller served as a successful U-Boat commander in the German Navy in the First World War. After the war he trained as a Protestant minister and was ordained in 1924. He was always a German nationalist and indeed welcomed the arrival of the Nazis in power as he hoped it would lead to revival of his country's fortunes.

However, he was not a racist, and in 1933 objected to the Reich Church's 'Aryan paragraph', which stated that Christians of Jewish descent, or married to 'non-Aryans', could not be ministers. In 1934 he joined a group of other Protestants, including Dietrich Bonhöffer, at Barmen in setting up the Confessional Church. At this stage they were just objecting to what they saw as Nazi interference in their church. However, Niemöller really did not understand what he was up against. In 1936 he wrote a strong protest against Nazi interference and anti-Semitism. He was arrested and kept in concentration camps from 1938 until 1945.

On his release he signed the Stuttgart Declaration, 1945, saying that he could have done more to oppose the Nazis.

GESTAPO SECRET FILE

OPPOSITION GROUPS
3 Army officers

SUPPORT: A group of army officers.

AIMS: To replace Hitler and seize power.

ACTIVITIES: Attempting to assassinate Hitler.

WHEN MOST ACTIVE: 1943–1944

Source 2

◀ Hitler's bombed conference room, July 1944

What happened...

Many upper-class Germans were scornful of Hitler, with his lower-class origins and street-fighting past. They had supported the Kaiser and traditionally served in the army, as officers. Hitler bought the support of the army in 1934 by weakening the SA in the Night of the Long Knives (page 49). However, Hitler's racial policies horrified many of the officer class. Many of them were against Hitler's rush to war in 1939 and opposed the invasion of the USSR in 1941. They were horrified by the brutal actions of the SS in eastern Europe, which were against their strict code of honour in war. They also resented

Hitler meddling in military strategy. When victory turned to defeat in 1943, they decided that Hitler had to be removed.

There were said to be dozens of plots to assassinate Hitler. The one that came nearest to success was organised by Claus von Stauffenberg, who planted a bomb in Hitler's military headquarters in July 1944. It went off, but Hitler was not killed. Hitler used the failed plot to round up all his known opponents, whether they were part of the bomb plot or not. As a result 5000 people were arrested and executed.

GESTAPO SECRET FILE

OPPOSITION GROUPS
4 Young people: Edelweiss Pirates

SUPPORT: Working-class young people. Not a united organisation, but local groups going their own way. Impossible to say how many are involved – a few hundred young people in each big city at the most.

AIMS: Avoiding Hitler Youth meetings and having fun.

ACTIVITIES: Meeting up to sing songs making fun of Hitler, the Nazis and the Hitler Youth. Having sex. Drinking. Wearing badges of the edelweiss (a white alpine flower), or skull and crossbones. Some groups wear check shirts, black shorts and white socks. Some groups are quite political and beat up Nazis.

WHEN MOST ACTIVE: 1938–1944

Source 3

▲ An Edelweiss Pirate group who called themselves 'The Navajos'

What happened...

Youth groups like the Edelweiss Pirates infuriated the Nazis because they rejected the whole Nazi idea. In 1944 a Hitler Youth leader in Cologne was killed so some Edelweiss Pirates were hanged in revenge.

GESTAPO SECRET FILE

OPPOSITION GROUPS
5 Young people: the White Rose Group

SUPPORT: A small group of students at Munich University led by Hans Scholl, Sophie Scholl and Christoph Probst.

AIMS: To shame the German people by protesting against the Nazis. To urge Germans to sabotage the war effort and overthrow Hitler.

ACTIVITIES: Spreading anti-Nazi messages through handing out leaflets, putting up posters and writing graffiti on walls.

WHEN MOST ACTIVE: Summer 1942; Jan–Feb 1943

Source 4

▲ The White Rose Group (left to right: Hans Scholl, Sophie Scholl, Christoph Probst)

What happened...

The White Rose Group were disgusted at the lack of opposition to the Nazis and their persecution of the Jews. Sophie Scholl wrote: 'Germany's name will be disgraced forever unless German youth finally rises up, takes revenge, smashes its torturers and builds a new, spiritual Europe'. Hans and Sophie were arrested and tortured before being executed (see page 69).

Source 5

From a White Rose leaflet, written in 1942

Our present state is a dictatorship of evil. Why not rise up? Sabotage armaments and war industry plants; sabotage meetings, festivals, anything the Nazis have created.

Source 6

Article in a German newspaper, 22 February 1943

On 22 February 1943, the People's Court sentenced to death the following persons: Hans Scholl, aged 24; Sophie Scholl, aged 21. The sentence was carried out the same day. Typical outsiders, these two people shamelessly committed offences against the security of Germany, by painting slogans on houses and distributing leaflets. At this time of heroic struggle on the part of the German people, these despicable criminals deserve a speedy and dishonourable death.

Source 7

Extract from a radio programme broadcast on 27 June 1943 by the famous German writer, Thomas Mann, whilst in exile in Britain. Thomas Mann left Germany in 1933

Hans and Sophie Scholl, put their heads on the block for the love of Germany. They went to their death after telling the judge at court to his face that 'soon you will be standing here where we now stand'. Good splendid young people! You shall not have died in vain; you shall not be forgotten. The Nazis have built monuments to common killers in Germany – but the German revolution will tear them down and replace them with people like you.

Source 8

Extract from a leaflet issued by the National Committee for a Free Germany

A short time ago we heard the terrible news that two young Germans, Hans and his sister Sophie Scholl, were executed at the end of February. They belonged to a group of noble and courageous young Germans who refused to put up with the terrible sufferings of Nazi Germany any longer. They were the first to raise the flag of freedom. The axe of the Hitler executioner was raised two times; two times it fell; and two young heads rolled from the block. Two heroes died, but their struggle for German freedom lives on in the hearts of millions of young Germans.

Discuss

1 Why do you think Source 6 portrays Hans and Sophie Scholl differently from Sources 7 and 8?

2 What do you think the Scholls meant when they said to the judge 'soon you will be standing here where we now stand' (Source 7)?

3 In Source 7 Thomas Mann says that a monument to the Scholls should be built.
   a) Do you agree?
   b) Do any of the other opposition groups you have studied deserve to be remembered in this way?
   Discuss this idea and then prepare a five-minute presentation on your choice.

Why didn't Germans oppose the Nazis?

Look back over the five groups of opponents and the danger rating you gave them for the Activity on page 64. Compare your scores with others in the class. Did you give anyone the highest rating? Probably not!

One of the hardest things to explain when you study Nazi Germany is why there was not more opposition. This is what you are going to work on now. Start with these four ordinary Germans and their answers to the question: 'Why don't I oppose the Nazis?'

Activity

You are going to create your own diagram to sum up the reasons why opposition to the Nazis was so weak.

1 Write Wilhelm's name in the middle of a piece of paper. Write the words 'Terror', 'Isolation', 'Nazi achievements' and 'Propaganda' around his name.
2 Read what Wilhelm says. How important do you think each of these four factors was in explaining Wilhelm's failure to oppose the Nazis? Draw lines between Wilhelm and the factors. Use a thick, bold line for the most important factor, and a thin, faint or dotted line for less important factors.

Propaganda   Nazi achievements

WILHELM

Terror   Isolation

3 Look for links between the factors. Draw links between factors, using thick and bold or thin and faint lines depending on how strong you think the links were.
4 Now draw three more charts for Hermann, Maria and Kitty.

I don't like the Nazis, but I'm scared to say so to anyone else. I know exactly what happens to those who do: the Gestapo calls on them one night and they disappear.

They get beaten to death in the police station, or on the way there, or in a concentration camp. I daren't say what I think. The local Nazi boss – a dreadful fat lout, used to be a butcher's assistant, no manners at all – knows I don't like them. He's looking for a chance to get me. He even offered one of my servants a thousand marks for any information which could lead to my arrest. My beautiful Germany has been over-run by these pigs! But I've got my estate to manage and my family and servants to think of. I really dare not speak out.

Wilhelm

Sometimes I get worried about what the Nazis are doing, but then when I hear them explain things it all makes sense again.

My older brother is in the Hitler Youth and gets to go to big torchlight rallies: he says it's a wonderful experience, swept along by the huge crowd all working for the same thing. It's on the radio too: my mum and I listen to Goebbels telling us all the great things Hitler and the Nazis have done and how they're going to make Germany even better. Of course, some bad people have been locked up, but Hitler says they deserved it – and I trust Hitler. My dad reads the papers and he says, 'Why should we want to change things when the Nazis are getting everything right? We had all that argument under Weimar and look where it got us.'

Hermann

I like the Nazis. I think Hitler is the best thing that has happened to Germany for years.

Look what the Nazis have achieved. Look how they have built up our army and navy again. Other countries won't be putting us down so much now! And unemployment – those layabouts are being made to work instead of living off the dole. There's order on the streets now – none of the noise and violence we had to put up with under that awful Weimar Government. The Nazis are organised and focused and Hitler is the strong man we need. Of course, to set Germany straight again has meant taking a firm line with some people, like those Communists who want a revolution here, as in the USSR. They deserve to be locked up. So do all the other bad elements Hitler has removed.

WHY DON'T I OPPOSE THE NAZIS?

Maria

I hate the Nazis but what can I do? Since the other political parties have been banned there is nowhere to turn. I feel like I am on my own.

I used to read the Socialist newspaper, but it stopped soon after the Nazis took over. The Socialist rallies and meetings I used to go to don't happen any more. Most of the great speakers, organisers and leaders we used to rely on have gone. Many have died in those awful Nazi camps. There are some old friends I can talk to, of course. We have a grumble and crack a few jokes. But I'm not a heroine: I can't go underground, or sabotage the war factories, much as I'd like to. I wouldn't know how, and I've got my old mother and three children to look after. But we're not going to get rid of Hitler by cracking anti-Nazi jokes. There's no one to lead us any more. We feel so weak, useless and disorganised.

Kitty

Meet the Examiner: Developing effective explanations

Why was opposition to the Nazis so weak? [12]

You may use the following in your answer and any other information of your own:

- July 1933 All opposition parties closed down
- 1936 All Church youth groups closed down
- 1943 White Rose Group members executed

You will meet this kind of question as Question 3 or 4 on your exam paper. You will have a simple choice: answer just one of the two questions. With 12 marks, it is quite an important question. You will need to make a plan before you start and spend about 18 minutes on the whole question.

This is obviously a 'WHY?' question and a 'WHY?' question means that you need to write an explanation, not a description. The question here does **not** say 'Describe the main groups who opposed the Nazis'. It asks you to explain the reasons why they were so weak.

Note the word **reasons**. There is bound to be more than one reason for a big question like this one.

How to write effective explanations

Step 1: Identify a range of reasons

You could start with the reasons Wilhelm, Kitty, Hermann and Maria give on pages 70 and 71.

Step 2: Use connectives to tie in what you know to the question

Do not just give a reason why opposition was weak: **prove it!**
You can do this by using good **connectives** such as:

This meant that...
This resulted in...
This led to...

Activity

Look at this answer. The student has used what Hermann says on page 71 to write a first paragraph. The student has also used connectives to link this reason with an explanation of why opposition to the Nazis was so weak.

> One reason why opposition to the Nazis was so weak was that in the years after 1933 they were quite popular.

The student identifies a reason: the popularity of the Nazis

> Many Germans were pleased that the Nazis were building up the German armed forces again, dealing with unemployment, and bringing law and order.

The student supports this reason with some good details.

> This meant that the opponents of the Nazis found it hard to gain support and their opposition was weak as a result.

The student ties this reason to the question.

Activity

That's one paragraph done.

Now have a go yourself at writing another paragraph which explains another reason. You could use what Wilhelm, Maria and Kitty say on pages 70 and 71. Don't forget to use connectives to **prove** your argument!

Make connections

Section 2.3 is about opposition, but Section 2.2 was about a related topic: Nazi control by terror and propaganda. Look back over that section to remind yourself of the key points. What material from that section could you use to help answer this question? Knowledge from one topic can be very useful in answering a question on another topic. In fact, the ability to pull in information from different parts of the course is what examiners are looking for to award top level marks.

Step 3: Structure your conclusion so that it analyses the factors

Your conclusion is important. It should be short and go back to the wording in the question. It should not be a detailed summary of everything you've ever written.

Start by showing that several reasons were involved. Make it clear which reason you think was most important.

Support your argument for this key reason. For example:

> Opposition to the Nazis was weak because they were popular; people, especially young people, were indoctrinated; opposition views were not heard; and opponents were removed.
> The most important reason why opposition was weak was that the Nazis treated opponents very harshly, removing leaders and terrorising their supporters. With no leaders and no means of getting their ideas across, opposition to the Nazis was bound to be weak.

3.1 Did the Nazis change the lives of everyone in Germany?

Hitler had very clear ideas about how everyone fitted into his Nazi future. Young people, women and workers had important roles but Jews and others soon discovered that they had no place in Nazi society. You will find out about some of these people and decide how much the Nazis really changed people's lives.

My name is Hans and I'm thirteen years old. I live in a small town with my parents and my younger sister, Anna. I like playing with my friends, although I wish there was more for us to do here. I'm trying to do well at school; times are hard and my father has just lost his job so I want to be able to get work when I grow up. I'm hearing the grown-ups talk a lot about Hitler these days, but I don't suppose he'll make much difference to my life.

Hans

Life in Germany, 1933

Here are four Germans, talking about themselves in 1933. Hitler has just become ruler of Germany.

I'm Karl and I live in Dortmund. I'm a metal worker. I've got twenty years' experience at a lathe, so I know what I'm doing. Or I would, if I had a job. Like millions of others I'm out of work now and I hate seeing my family scraping by on unemployment benefits. I didn't vote for Hitler. I can't see that he's going to be able to pull Germany out of this mess.

Karl

Gudrun

My name is Lisa and I'm starting university next year. I'm Jewish. My family have lived here, in Frankfurt, for centuries. My father fought for our country in the war and was gassed, so he can't work much. I'm a bit scared by some of the things Hitler says about the Jews and I could hardly believe it when a man like that became Chancellor. But my Granny says, 'The soup's not served as hot as it's cooked.' I hope she's right.

Lisa

My name is Gudrun and I live in Berlin. I'm a senior hospital doctor. After the war, when the Weimar Republic replaced the old Kaiser's rule, the situation for women improved a lot. We got the vote, equal pay and equal rights at work. There were much better opportunities for women to make a career. I'm married, but my husband and I decided to have just one child so that I could get back to work. I've heard Hitler ranting his old-fashioned views on women but I can't think he's really going to put the clock back.

Hitler's Germany

Hitler had very clear ideas about the kind of Germany he wanted.

A Germany with the Nazi Party in control
It was not the job of the German people to vote, or criticise; they had simply to obey and be grateful.

A racially pure Germany
Only Aryans – the blond-haired, blue-eyed and pale-skinned – would be welcome.

A Germany with traditional roles for men and women
Women, wearing simple clothes and no make-up, would stay at home, cook simple meals and produce babies.
Men would work and, if necessary, fight.
Boys and girls would be prepared for their different roles through the education system.

▲ A Nazi propaganda poster from the 1930s. At the top it says: 'The NSDAP (Nazi Party) protects the national community.' At the bottom it says: 'People: if you need help, go to your local Party group.'

Discuss

1 What does Source 1 tell you about each of the three big Nazi ideas:
   a) racial purity
   b) traditional roles for men and women
   c) the role of the Nazi Party?
2 What else does it suggest to you about Nazi rule?

Activity

Look again at the four Germans on the opposite page. Copy and complete a table, like this one, to show how the Nazi ideas might change each person's life.
1 In the first column, write three points about the life of each person in 1933.
2 How do you think their lives might change under Nazi rule? Put these ideas in column 2.
3 Which person do you think is going to be affected most by Nazi rule?
You should leave column 3 blank for now. Fill that in later as you work through the next eight pages.

	Their lives in 1933	Your prediction: changes likely in their lives under Nazi rule	What really happened
Hans			
Karl			
Gudrun			
Lisa			

How did the Nazis change the lives of young people?

Hans

1939

Source 2

Hitler's words on youth, from *Hitler Speaks* by Herman Rauschning, 1939
In my great educational work I am beginning with the young. My magnificent youngsters! With them I can make a new world!
My teaching is hard. Weakness has to be knocked out of them. The world will shrink in alarm from the youngsters who grow up in my schools: a violent, masterful, brave, cruel, younger generation. I will have no intellectual training. Knowledge is ruin to my young men.

The Nazis put a massive effort into getting us young people on their side. They knew they would never get the support of all adults, but if they could control young people they would control the future...

The Hitler Youth

Source 3

◀ Hitler Youth members jumping over fire to demonstrate their bravery

The Hitler Youth was a successful movement even before the Nazis came to power, with 30 per cent of all young Germans already members. Once the Nazis were in power membership became hard to avoid, with over 80 per cent of young Germans as members by 1939. Each member swore a personal oatah of loyalty to Hitler.

Hitler Youth members spent their time doing physical activities, such as hiking, running and jumping, doing Nazi charity work and listening to lectures. To become members boys had to: run 60 metres in twelve seconds, jump 2.75 metres, throw a ball 25 metres, complete a one-and-a-half-day cross-country march, do close combat exercises, jump out of a first floor window wearing full army battledress and answer questions on Nazi ideas and history. For girls the emphasis was on keeping fit and home-building.

In schools

The whole curriculum was used to teach what the Nazis wanted young people to think. Teachers who refused to teach these things were sacked.

PE: Three double lessons a week for boys and girls. Boxing was compulsory for boys. Girls were taught home-making and childcare.

History: Pupils were taught all about the unfair Treaty of Versailles, the rise of the Nazis and the wickedness of Jews and Communists. No earlier German history or history of other countries was taught.

Biology: Pupils were instructed on the Nazi racial ideas of the superiority of the 'Aryan race'.

German: Lessons focused on German war heroes and the Nazi Party.

Geography: Pupils were taught about the lands that had once been German and should now be re-taken.

Maths: Source 5 shows how Nazi ideas were put to use.

Source 5

Extract from a Nazi maths textbook

To keep a mentally ill person costs 4 marks a day. There are 300,000 mentally ill people in care.

a) How much do these people cost the state?

b) How many marriage loans [see page 80] of 1000 marks each could be made from this money?

Source 4

▲ Javelin throwers in the League of German Maidens

During the war

After 1943, as the war turned against him, Hitler called on Hitler Youth members to carry out duties such as collecting scrap metal and clothes for the troops, and charity donations for war widows and those made homeless by bombing. Later, thousands of recruits, some as young as 17, 16, even 15, joined up to fight for their Führer. By the end, in 1945, boys as young as 12 were given weapons and ordered to fight.

HOWEVER...

Many young people hated the Hitler Youth and one in five young Germans never joined. They found the propaganda talks boring and repetitive. They disliked being bossed about. Some joined actively anti-Nazi groups like the Edelweiss Pirates (see page 68). Many resented having to give up their studies to go on weekend camps – see what Hitler says about education in the last two sentences of Source 1. Universities complained about falling academic standards.

Activity

1   Look back to Hans in 1933 on page 74. How do you think Nazi rule would have affected his life? In column 3 of your table list the changes that took place.

2   Mark each change out of 5 for how serious you think it is (5 very serious, 1 trivial).

3   Did any of the changes make things better for Hans?

How did the Nazis change the lives of workers?

Karl

Source 6

Robert Ley, Head of the German Labour Front, speaking in May 1933
Without the German worker there is no German nation … Workers, I swear to you that we shall not only preserve everything which exists, we shall build up even further the protection of the worker's rights, so that he can enter the new National Socialist state as a worthwhile and respected member of the nation.

How did the Nazis reduce unemployment?

The Minister of the Economy, Hjalmar Schacht, introduced his 'New Plan'.

- **By a huge building programme.** New motorways (autobahns), schools, hospitals and houses were built and paid for by the government.
- **By increasing the armed forces from 100,000 to 1,400,000.** All males aged 18–25 had to do two years' military service.
- **By re-arming Germany.** New tanks, aeroplanes, guns and battleships were ordered. Industries of all kinds, especially steel, boomed and millions of jobs were created to build these weapons.
- **By putting young men to work.** All male 18–25 year-olds did six months in the National Labour Service (RAD), doing things like planting trees or digging ditches. They were given food and lodging, but paid only pocket money.
- **By removing many women from the employment register** (see pages 80–81).
- **By removing many Jews from the employment register** (see page 83).

I was one of 6 million out of work in Germany in 1933. The Nazis promised to solve this problem and they did. Millions of jobs were created by rebuilding the armed forces. Women and Jews were removed from the unemployment figures. By 1939 unemployment was down to only 300,000 and there was actually a shortage of workers.

Source 7

▲ Workers ready to start work on building the first motorway, 1933

How were the workers treated?

Trade unions and all workers' organisations were abolished. All workers had to join the German Labour Front (DAF), run by the Nazis. The Labour Front organised some improvements to workers' lives. They negotiated better conditions at work: better lunches, new toilets, etc. Through an organisation called 'Strength Through Joy', they also arranged leisure activities for workers and their families. These included holidays (see Source 9), film-shows, concerts, hiking, keep-fit clubs and sporting fixtures. Millions of workers and their families took part.

▲ Young men in the National Labour Service (RAD)

Source 9

▲ Robert Ley (see Source 6) with holidaymakers on a 'Strength Through Joy' cruiseship

HOWEVER...

Workers had no rights. The Labour Front did what employers asked. As a result, wages were lower and hours longer than before the Nazis came to power. The Nazis wanted to support farmers, so gave them good prices for the food they produced. However, this meant that food prices for city workers rose. With lower wages and higher prices, workers were actually worse off, in real terms, than before the Depression. By 1937, average families were eating less wheat bread, meat, bacon, milk, eggs, fish, vegetables, sugar, tropical fruit and beer compared to the 1927 figures. Their only increase was in amounts of rye bread, cheese and potatoes.

Everyone had to work and skilled men could be sent to do heavy labour on schemes like autobahn building. People who refused to work under these conditions could be arrested and sent to forced labour camps. Young men in the RAD earned almost no money and were treated as if they were in the army, as you can see in Source 8.

Activity

1   Look back to Karl in 1933 on page 74. How do you think Nazi rule would have affected his life? In column 3 of your table list the changes that took place.
2   Mark each change out of 5 for how serious you think it is (5 very serious, 1 trivial).
3   Did any of the changes make things better for Karl?

How did the Nazis change the lives of women?

Gudrun

1939

> ## Source 10
>
> **Hitler, speaking in 1934 at a Nazi Party conference**
> Woman has her battlefield too; with each child that she brings into the world, she is fighting her fight on behalf of the nation.

'I have given a child to the Führer!' These are the words I heard a German woman call out after giving birth. This was just what Hitler wanted from women like me.

The Nazis were very old-fashioned in their attitude to women. They wanted women to be mothers not workers. These are some of the methods they used to try to achieve this.

Out!

All women employed by the state – doctors, civil servants and many teachers – were sacked. In appointing new staff, men were preferred to women.

Loans

Loans were offered to couples to encourage them to get married. They received 1000 marks, or about a half year's pay. The more children they had, the less they had to pay back. If they had four children they paid nothing back. But there was one condition: the woman had to leave her job.

Medals

Medals were awarded for having children: gold for eight; silver for six; bronze for four (see Source 11).

However, not everyone was allowed to have children. It was compulsory for women with inherited diseases, or weaknesses such as colour-blindness, to be sterilised.

Propaganda

In line with their old-fashioned ideas the Nazis also wanted women to wear simple, rather than fashionable clothes. Wearing trousers or high heels, having permed or dyed hair, using make-up or smoking in public were all frowned upon. Some Nazis got restaurants to ban women from smoking and 'good Nazis' were encouraged to tell off any fashionably-dressed women in public.

Slimming was also frowned upon as the Nazis wanted women to be strong and solid in order to have lots of babies.

Since it is not easy to pass laws about many of these things, the Nazis tried to persuade women to follow their ideals by using massive amounts of propaganda, such as leaflets (Source 12) and posters (Source 1 on page 75 and Source 13). Women were urged to follow the 'Three Ks': Kinder, Kirche, Küche (children, church, cooking).

Source 11

▲ The 'Honour Cross of the German Mother'

Source 12

From a Nazi leaflet issued to young German women

1 Remember that you are a German!
2 If you are healthy, do not stay single!
3 Keep your body pure!
4 Keep your mind and spirit pure!
5 Marry only for love!
6 As a German, choose only a husband of the same blood!
7 In choosing a husband, ask about his forebears [ancestors]!
8 Health is essential to beauty!
9 Don't look for a playmate but for a companion!
10 You should want to have as many children as possible!

Activity

1 The Nazi campaign to force women to follow their ideals was based on 'sticks and carrots'; that is, sticks to punish them if they did undesirable things and carrots to encourage them to do what the Nazis wanted. Which of the measures described here are 'sticks' and which are 'carrots'?
2 Choose the opposite point of view to the Nazis on one of these topics. Design a poster to persuade women to agree with you.
3 Look back to Gudrun in 1933 on page 74. How do you think Nazi rule would have affected her life? In column 3 of your table list the changes that took place.
4 Mark each change out of 5 for how serious you think it is (5 very serious, 1 trivial).
5 Did any of the changes make things better for Gudrun?

Source 13

▲ A Nazi poster from 1935. It says: 'Germany grows through strong mothers and healthy children'

HOWEVER...

Women did not give up their jobs easily. Although the number of marriages and babies born went up, so did the number of women working. The economy was booming so employers wanted workers, especially women, who could be paid less than men.

This division over Nazi policies towards women became more serious in the war. The war effort brought a huge demand for more workers. Unlike in Britain, where women were conscripted into war work from the beginning, the Nazis were very reluctant to abandon their views on women's role. Workers from the lands the Nazis had conquered in 1940–1941 were forcibly sent to work in Germany. Many German companies used the slave labour of the concentration camps.

Not until 1943, as the war turned against Germany, were all women aged 17–45 called up to work in factories and munitions. Those who did were mainly working-class women; many middle-class women refused. Germany was in difficulties by then, with massive air raids causing terrible destruction of cities and disruption of daily life. There were food shortages. In this situation, with the men away at war, many women chose to stay at home to carry out the difficult and time-consuming job of looking after their families.

How did the Nazis change the lives of people who did not 'fit'?

Source 1 on page 75 shows the people the Nazi Party wanted in their Germany. But what if you did not fit?

Several types of people failed to meet the Nazi ideal. It was soon very clear that there was no place in Nazi Germany for these 'undesirables'.

UNDESIRABLES

- *Those who **wouldn't** work.* Habitual criminals, tramps, beggars, alcoholics and others like them were regarded as socially useless. They were rounded up in 1933 and 500,000 of them were sent to concentration camps.

- *Those who **couldn't** work.* The physically disabled and mentally ill were also regarded as a burden. From 1938 onwards the Nazis began to put such people to death in gas chambers. Around 350,000 men and women who were said to produce 'inferior' offspring, or who carried inherited conditions, were compulsorily sterilised.

- *Those who did not fit into 'normal' families.* This included homosexuals, who were savagely persecuted. About 15,000 were arrested and sent to concentration camps. Many were castrated or used in medical experiments. Himmler was shocked to discover several homosexuals in the SS. He ordered them to be sent to a camp where they were 'shot while trying to escape'.

- *Those who would not make Hitler their first loyalty.* Socialists and Communists refused to do this for political reasons; Jehovah's Witnesses for religious reasons. All were put in concentration camps.

- *Those who were not 'Aryans'.* This included black people, Gypsies and Jews. Some 385 black Germans were compulsorily sterilised. Gypsies were harassed for two reasons: they were not Aryans and they did not do ordinary work. Gypsies were put in concentration camps and around 500,000 were later killed in the death camps.

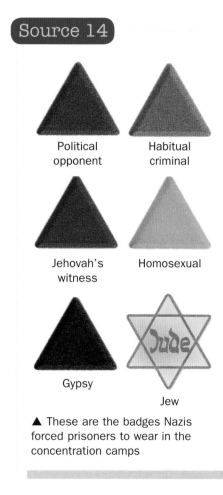

Source 14

Political opponent

Habitual criminal

Jehovah's witness

Homosexual

Gypsy

Jew

▲ These are the badges Nazis forced prisoners to wear in the concentration camps

Activity

1 Look at the six groups of people represented in Source 14. Explain why each group was 'undesirable' to the Nazis.
2 Are all of these groups accepted as full members of society today? Are there any other groups who do not have full citizenship rights?

From prejudice to persecution

Jews had suffered religious prejudice for centuries. But the Nazis took anti-Semitism to a new extreme. They used bogus research to suggest that Jews were an 'inferior' race. They blamed the Jews for the problems in Germany. They encouraged ordinary Germans to hate Jews. Gradually, they took away the civil rights of German Jews.

Lisa

In 1933 there were half a million Jews in Germany. We were only about 1 per cent of the population. Not many, you might think. But Hitler was obsessed. He went after us with all the power and resources the modern German state could provide.

Before 1933
- Nazis encouraged boycott of Jewish-owned shops.
- Anti-Jewish graffiti scrawled on shop windows.
- SA stood outside Jewish businesses to threaten shoppers.

1933
- Jewish lawyers and judges dismissed.
- Jews banned from all public service jobs, such as teachers and civil servants.
- Non-Aryan children forbidden from playing with Aryan children.

1935
- Jewish writers not published.
- Jewish musicians barred from playing in state orchestras.
- Jews only allowed to sit on park-benches labelled 'For Jews'.

    The Nuremberg Laws
    Jews could not be German citizens.
    Jews could not marry, or have sex with, non-Jews.

1936
- Jews not allowed to own typewriters or bicycles.
- Anti-Jewish posters temporarily removed during Berlin Olympics.

1938
- Jews not allowed to practise as doctors.
- Jews not allowed to run their own businesses.
- Jewish children barred from state schools.
- Jews banned from swimming-pools, cinemas, theatres and concert halls.
- Male Jews had to add the name 'Israel' and females the name 'Sarah' to their own.

Kristallnacht – In November, 1938, a young Jewish student, angry at the treatment of Jews in Germany, shot a German diplomat in Paris. In retaliation, Nazi leaders encouraged their supporters to attack German Jews and smash up their homes, shops and synagogues. The police were instructed not to intervene. After two nights of violence (on 9–10 November) 91 Jews lay dead. Many streets in Germany were strewn with broken glass. The event became known as Kristallnacht – 'Crystal night' or 'The night of broken glass'. In the following months 30,000 German Jews were arrested and taken to concentration camps. It was a turning-point in the Nazi treatment of Jews; soon life for them was going to get very much worse.

1939
- Jews not allowed to work as dentists, chemists or nurses.
- Jews not allowed out of their homes after 8 p.m. in winter, 9 p.m. in summer.
- Jews had to hand over any jewellery, gold or silver to the police.

This story continues in Section 3.2.

Activity

Complete the table on page 75 for Lisa.

Discuss

Look at the restrictions listed here. Which ones:
- were minor nuisances
- prevented Jewish children from having a normal childhood
- prevented Jews from earning a living
- were serious restrictions on Jews' rights as citizens of Germany?

Using charts to organise your revision

Making charts helps you to remember the key points.

Use the information from pages 80–81 to copy and complete this chart about how women's lives changed under the Nazis. Some boxes have already been filled in for you. Use the Results column to consider whether people's lives changed as much as the Nazis would have liked. The paragraph which starts 'However…' (page 81) will help you.

Women	Before the Nazis came to power	Changes made by the Nazis.	Results
Marriage		Women were put under pressure to get married – preferably to an Aryan man.	
Work	Women were encouraged to have their own careers.		
Children			
Fashion		Women encouraged to wear simple clothes: fashion discouraged.	

Make your own version of this chart for the other three groups of people in this section.

Using pictures to trigger your memory

Another way of organising, learning and remembering the changes in people's lives under the Nazis is to look at Hans, Gudrun, Karl and Lisa.

Here is Hans in 1933 and 1939. Fill in the boxes with notes about each aspect of Hans' life in 1933 and 1939.
Make and label your own sketches for Gudrun, Karl and Lisa in the same way.

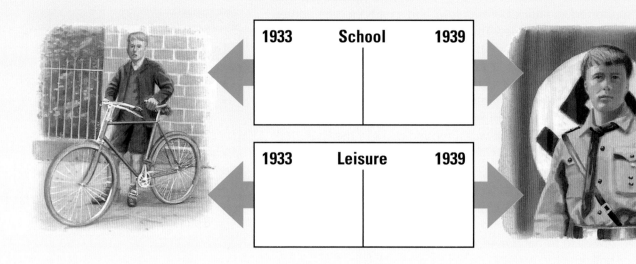

1933	School	1939

1933	Leisure	1939

> How did the lives of women in Germany change
> in the years 1933 to 1945?   [12]
>
> You may use the following in your answer and any other
> information of your own:
>
> • Women were urged to follow 'Kinder, Kirche, Küche'
>
> • Women were dismissed from state employment from
>   1934–1936
>
> • 1933 Loans of 1,000 marks offered to couples
>   on marriage

You could meet a question a bit like this as Question 3 or 4 on your exam paper. We have looked at examples of this kind of question on page 35, where we focused on the need to keep **relevant**, and on pages 50–51, where we showed how to use the three bullet points.

But this question is a little bit different: it is about **change**. Simply to describe women's lives under the Nazis is not enough! Change means saying something about the situation **before** as well as **after**. Only then can you prove whether anything changed.

What makes a good conclusion to a 'change' question?

1 Put forward a clear line of argument – your own final thoughts.

2 Don't write too much – aim to write less but think more!

To get top marks think about how much change. Look at the train below. In your answer, at which station will your train stop, and why?

3.2 The Holocaust

You saw, in Section 1.3, that Hitler's own anti-Semitism was deep-rooted. You saw, in Section 3.1, how the Nazis made life increasingly difficult for the Jews of Germany from the moment they took power in 1933. But the Second World War allowed the Nazis to push their anti-Jewish policy to new extremes.

The Einsatzgrüppen

In 1939, before the war, there were 350,000 Jews living in Nazi Germany. As the Nazis invaded first Poland, then the USSR, six million Jews came under their control. Following behind the invading armies were special SS squads, called Einsatzgrüppen. They rounded up Jews in each town, took them out into the country nearby and ordered them to dig a trench. The Jews were then shot and fell into the trench which became a mass grave.

The ghettos

Source 1

▲ Einsatzgrüppe soldier about to shoot a Jew at a mass grave in Vinnitsa, in what is now Ukraine, 1942

Source 2

▲ Young children in the Warsaw ghetto, 1941

In Poland, Czechoslovakia, Hungary and Lithuania, Jews were also forced into special sections of cities, called ghettos. The Warsaw ghetto, for example, held 400,000 Jews, 30 per cent of the population of the city, in a tiny area, surrounded by three-metre high walls. The ghettos were shut off from the rest of the city and were impossibly overcrowded. Food, water and power were cut off. Hundreds of Jews died there each day. Anyone who tried to leave was shot.

The 'Final Solution'

On 31 July 1941, Goering (the Economics Minister) ordered Himmler (the Head of the SS)and Heydrich (an SS general) to carry out the 'final solution' to the 'Jewish question' in Europe. Shooting (carried out by the Einsatzgrüppen) and the ghettos were seen as inefficient ways of killing millions of people. In January 1942 Nazi leaders held a Conference at Wannsee, near Berlin, to work out a more 'efficient' way of killing Jews. It was decided to bring in industrial methods. Six special death camps were built, with gas chambers capable of killing 2,000 people at once, and large ovens for disposing of the bodies.

All the death camps had good railway links, so Jews could be brought by train from all over Europe, a terrible journey of several days. Many died on the way. Auschwitz was one of these camps, and began killing people by the end of 1941. By the end of the war, 1,100,000 people had been killed in the Auschwitz gas chambers. The other camps were:

- **Treblinka:** at this tiny camp, only 600 metres by 400 metres, at least 850,000 Jews, mainly from Warsaw, but also from elsewhere in Europe, including Hungary and Greece, were killed, as well as over 2000 Gypsies and Roma.

- **Sobibor:** at least 300,000 Jews as well as thousands of Soviet prisoners of war were killed here.

- **Belzec:** at least 600,000 Jews, mainly from Poland, and several thousand Gypsies were killed here.

- **Majdenek:** 60,000 Jews from all over Europe, as well as non-Jewish Poles and Russians, were killed here.

- **Chelmno:** over 150,000 Jews were killed here.

(Note that these death camps were different from the 15 concentration camps, which the Nazis had used as early as 1933 to imprison their enemies. Concentration camps were not built to kill people – although many thousands did die in them, of brutality, disease and starvation.)

In every country the Nazis ruled, lists of Jews were drawn up. They were taken from their homes and put on trains.

On arrival at the camp inmates walked past a Nazi doctor who indicated whether they should go left or right: left to work, right to the gas chambers. About 80 per cent of arrivals were killed at once; those put to work normally lasted just a few months before dying of malnutrition and overwork.

By the end of the war some 6 million Jews had been murdered, as well as Gypsies, homosexuals and around 4 million Russian prisoners of war.

▲ Deportation of Jews from Wuerzburg, Germany, guarded by the police, 27 November 1941

▲ A gas chamber in Auschwitz death camp, 1942. The gas used was Zyklon B, a cyanide poison gas. It took up to 15 minutes to kill everybody – see Source 5 on the next page.

Source 5

An extract from the memoirs of Rudolph Höss, commandant of Auschwitz, written after his arrest. He was tried for war crimes and executed in 1947

Before entering the gas chamber, Jewish prisoners would tell them in their own language to leave their clothes neatly together and remember where they had put them.

The women went in first with the children, followed by the men … The door would be quickly screwed up and the gas released through vents in the ceiling. About one-third died straightaway. The remainder began to scream and struggle for air. The screaming, however, soon changed to the death rattle and in a few minutes all lay still. It took from three to fifteen minutes to kill everybody.

We usually waited about half-an-hour before we opened the doors. The bodies were then taken up by lift and laid in front of the ovens which had been stoked up. Up to three corpses could be put in each oven at the same time.

Source 6

▲ The entrance to the Auschwitz Death Camp, where more than one million people were killed during the Second World War. Note the train tracks leading right into the camp. Trains brought Jews to Auschwitz from all over Nazi-occupied Europe.

Discuss

Look at this list of people who helped to make the Holocaust happen:
- Hitler
- Hitler's henchmen, such as Himmler and Goebbels
- Camp commandants, such as Rudolph Höss (see Source 5)
- The SS camp doctors who made the selection
- The clerks who wrote the lists of Jews' names
- The police who rounded up the Jews
- The engine drivers who drove the trains to the camps
- The engineers who designed the gas chambers
- The builders who built the gas chambers
- The German people who did nothing to stop the killings
- Governments of other countries who didn't bomb the railway lines and camps.

1 Are all these people to blame?
2 Who is most to blame?
3 Who could have stopped the Holocaust?

HOWEVER…

Jews did fight against what was happening to them. Jewish resistance groups took to the countryside and armed uprisings took place in the ghettos. The Warsaw ghetto uprising of 1943 lasted 43 days against the German army. There were also uprisings at the camps. In October 1943, 600 Jews escaped from Sobibor camp in Poland.

Conclusion

The overall picture: what have you learned?

Activity

Imagine you are an assistant editor working on a new edition of this book. You have decided to improve it. There are various jobs to do. You could either do all of them yourself or work in groups with one person, or pair, working on each task.

TASK 1
You want an illustrated **contents page**.
a) You should now have an image for each of the nine enquiries (see page 2).
b) Write a short caption to go with each picture.
c) Briefly - in one sentence for each - justify your choice of pictures.

TASK 2
You want a new **front cover picture**.
a) Look at the one we chose. Discuss whether you think it is a good choice.
b) Now over to you. Decide on one image for the front cover of your book.
c) Write a paragraph to explain why this is a good choice.

TASK 3
You want to put a **quotation or a poem** on the title page of the book which says something important about this book.
a) Choose a quotation or a poem.
b) Explain why you think this is a good way to start the book.

TASK 4
You want a new 'blurb' for the back cover. It should outline what the book is about and why it is important.
a) Draft your 'blurb'. It should be no more than 100 words.
b) Compare your blurb with a partner's. Agree on a blurb text together.

This book has suggested some strategies you could use to help you revise. Here is a reminder of them. When you come to revise, remember that each one can be used for any topic.

Linking factors

In the Activity on page 17 you saw students becoming a 'Human Plan' of how the problems of the Weimar Republic linked together. You could use an Activity like this to explore links between factors in other events in this depth study.

Acronyms

We used a LAMB on page 19 to help you remember the terms of the Treaty of Versailles. You also made your own acronym to remember the problems faced by the Weimar Republic. Here is another one to sum up Hitler's BIG ideas for how Germany should be ruled.

Blood –   Hitler believed that only those of 'pure German **blood**' should be part of the Master Race. This idea led to the persecution of the Jews and, eventually, the Holocaust.

Invasion –   Hitler thought that Germany should **invade** other countries in order to provide 'living space' for the growing German population. This idea led to the Second World War.

Government – Hitler believed in strong **government**. This led to the destruction of democracy and the establishment of a dictatorship.

Activity 1

1 The best acronyms are the ones you make up yourself. If you create it yourself it is easier to remember. Work in pairs. Invent an acronym to help you remember another topic, for example the reasons why opposition to the Nazis was weak (see pages 70–71). Vote in class on the best acronym.

Memory maps

Memory maps are an excellent way to summarise your notes and boost your memory. On pages 20–21 you produced a memory map to summarise the problems faced by the Weimar Republic. You can use memory maps to summarise other key topics.

Activity 2

2 Use the advice on pages 20–21 to produce a memory map that summarises how Hitler used terror and propaganda to control Germany (see section 2.2). You could start like this:

Charts

On page 84 you used a chart to bring together and analyse the changes to various people's lives in Nazi Germany. Other charts were used on pages 24, 52, 64 and 75. Once you have completed them, they become useful revision material.

On page 84; pages 24, 52, 64 and 75

Activity 3

3 Take one of the charts from the pages listed above and delete most of the boxes.
4 Test a friend by seeing how many of the blank boxes they can fill in.
5 Check their answers against the original.
6 Now swap roles and see how much of a nearly-blank chart you can fill in.

Living graphs

Living graphs can help summarise topics in a way that actively engages your brain. Look at the living graph you produced on page 47 to explore how Hitler became a dictator. Most students would find it easier to remember that in an exam than a list of bullet points. You could use a similar method to sort out the key points in Sections 1.3 and 1.4.

page 47

Activity 4

7 Produce a living graph like this which plots the popularity of the Nazi Party from 1919 to 1933.
8 Produce a living graph which plots the popularity of the Weimar Republic from 1919 to 1933.
9 Compare the two graphs. What pattern can you see?

You could also convert this into a 'walking graph'. Mark out the graph on the floor and you and your class become the graph. Your teacher can tell you how to do this. It is often easier to remember something active that you have done.

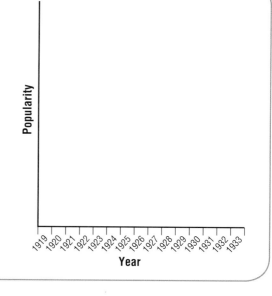

Examination questions are not as hard as they first look. The examiners are not trying to catch you out: they are trying to give you a chance to show what you know – **and what you can do with what you know**.

To make sure you answer the question on the paper and not the one you wish had turned up, you will need to practise how to 'de-code' questions.

Step 1 Read the question a couple of times.

Step 2 Highlight each of the following. You could use a different colour for each:

a) Content focus What topic the examiner wants you to focus on.

b) Date boundaries Stick to these carefully otherwise you will waste time writing about events that are not relevant to the question.

c) Question type Different question types require different approaches. Look for key words, like 'Why' or 'How far', that will help you work out what type of approach is needed.

d) Marks available Look at how many marks the question is worth. This gives you a guide as to how much you are expected to write.

e) Bullets Some questions include helpful items as bullet points.

Activity

Choose three exam questions from past papers. Your teacher will know where to find them. Identify the content focus, date boundaries, question type and marks available.

Look at the following question.

a) The content focus for this question is the growth in support for the Nazi Party.

b) The date boundaries are 1929–1932. This is important. An event such as the Reichstag Fire which occurred in 1933 should not be included in this answer. Nor should the Munich Putsch of 1923.

> Why did support for the Nazi Party grow between 1929 and 1932? [12]
> You may use the following in your answer and any other information of your own:
> • 1929 Wall Street Crash
> • 1930–1932 support for the Communists doubled from 54 seats in the Reichstag to nearly 100
> • 1932 Nazis become largest party in the Reichstag

c) The word 'Why' indicates that this is a causation-type question. You need to explain why support for the Nazis grew. Describing the Nazis' rise in support is not an answer.

d) There are twelve available marks. This indicates that the examiner expects a longer essay-style answer. This question is definitely worth planning carefully.

How are you going to include the bullet-point items in your answer?

Glossary

allies countries that have signed an agreement to support each other

anti-Semitism hatred of Jews

armistice cease-fire agreement

Aryan Nazi word for the German 'race'

attribution information given with a historical source describing who produced it, when, why, etc.

constitution the rules that decide how a country is governed

Dawes Plan an agreement between the USA and European countries in 1924, drawn up for the USA by Charles Dawes. The plan organised US loans to revive European economies, especially that of Germany

democracy a system of government in which all adults have the right to vote for the government they want

emergency powers the right of the German President to act outside the normal rules of the constitution in a crisis

Enabling Act the Enabling Act was passed in 1933, giving Hitler power to act without consulting the Reichstag or the President

extremist parties groups holding extreme political views. In Germany at this time the Nazis and the Communists were extremist parties seeking to overthrow democracy

Freikorps organisation of armed ex-soldier volunteers

Führer the German word for leader. Hitler's title after the death of President Hindenburg in 1934

German Labour Front (DAF) an organisation set up by the Nazis to improve the lives of workers

hyper-inflation inflation is when money decreases in value, so more is needed to pay for the same things. Hyper-inflation is where this gets completely out of hand and prices rise by enormous amounts

Kaiser German Emperor (the last Kaiser's rule ended in 1918)

League of Nations set up in 1919 for the promotion of international peace and security. Germany was a member from 1926 to 1933

passive resistance opposing government action in non-violent ways, refusing to co-operate, staging strikes, etc.

proportional representation (PR) a system of elections in which the number of people elected for a party is in proportion to the number of votes for that party. It gives representation to minorities, who do not do well in the 'first past the post' system, which is used in Britain today. PR can lead to lots of small parties and unstable governments

putsch an armed uprising aimed at taking over the government

Reichstag German parliament

reparations compensation for the damage caused by the First World War demanded by the victorious Allies from Germany on the grounds that Germany was to blame for the war (by Article 231 of the Treaty of Versailles). The amount was fixed at £6.6 million in 1921 but nothing like this amount was ever paid

republic a state that has an elected head of state rather than a hereditary ruler

SA abbreviation for Stürm-Abteilung (Stormtroopers). The brown-shirted gangs set up by Hitler to protect his meetings and break up the meetings of opponents in the early days of the Nazi Party

SS abbreviation for Schutz Staffel (protection squad). Originally Hitler's private bodyguard, they wore black uniforms and swore a personal oath of loyalty to him

Wall Street Crash sudden fall in stock prices in June 1929 on the US stock exchange, in Wall Street, New York

Young Plan an agreement made between Germany and the Allies, named after US representative Young, to lower reparations and allow Germany to pay them back over a longer period

Index